HELENE CI

HELENE CIXOUS

A Politics of Writing

Morag Shiach

London and New York

First published 1991
by Routledge
11 New Fetter Lane, London EC4P 4EE

Simultaneously published in the USA and Canada
by Routledge
a division of Routledge, Chapman and Hall, Inc.
29 West 35th Street, New York, NY 10001

Typeset in 10/12pt Palatino by
Intype Ltd, London
Printed in Great Britain by
TJ Press (Padstow) Ltd, Padstow, Cornwall

British Library Cataloguing in Publication Data
Shiach, Morag
Hélène Cixous.
1. French literature
I. Title
848.91409

Library of Congress Cataloging in Publication Data
Shiach, Morag
Hélène Cixous : a politics of writing / Morag Shiach.
p. cm.
Includes bibliographical references.
1. Cixous, Hélène, 1937- —Criticism and interpretation.
2. Feminism and literature—France—History—20th century.
3. Politics and literature—France—History—20th century.
I.Title.
PQ2663.I9Z84 1991
848'.91409—dc20   91–9503
ISBN 0 415 01333 X
ISBN 0 415 01334 8 pbk

For Caroline

CONTENTS

ILLUSTRATIONS

ACKNOWLEDGEMENTS

I would like to thank Hélène Cixous and Marguerite Sandré for their generosity and their help. I am also grateful to Sissel Lie for several very productive discussions of Cixous's work. Michael Moriarty and Lisa Jardine have read and responded to earlier drafts of this book, making many helpful suggestions, for which I thank them. I would also like to acknowledge the Cambridge Feminist Reading Group, and the seminar series on Feminism and Psychoanalysis organized by Teresa Brennan, where many ideas relevant to this book were discussed.

Finally, I would like to thank the CNRS and the British Council for giving me the funding necessary to undertake research in Paris.

INTRODUCTION

Hélène Cixous is a contemporary French writer, critic, and
theorist, whose works span a number of genres and address
a wide range of problems which have preoccupied the disci-
plines of English and French Studies over the last twenty
years. In France she is best known as the author of a large
number of avant-garde fictions and theatrical texts. Her early
work has been placed in relation to the *nouveau roman*, with
its investigation of the materiality of writing, of the complexity
of subjectivity, and of the transgressive potential of the literary
text. In the 1970s she became increasingly identified with a
literary and philosophical project that aimed to explore the
relations between sexuality and writing: a project that might
also be seen as involving theorists such as Irigaray, Kristeva,
Derrida, and Barthes, as well as writers like Jean Genet and
Marguerite Duras. More recently, her work has focused on the
relations between ethical, linguistic, and historical structures,
through explorations of a variety of moments of historical
change and crisis.

In English Studies, however, the role of Cixous's writings
has been quite specific, and relatively distinct from this complex and continuing project. Her incorporation into the critical
language of English Studies has been almost entirely at the
level of 'theory'. A small number of her texts has been translated, and these texts have repeatedly been mobilized in support of, or as ammunition against, a reading of the relations
between gender and writing. 'The Laugh of the Medusa' and
'Sorties', two essays dating from the mid-1970s where Cixous
discusses the transgressive potential of writing and
the relations between sexuality and textuality, have been

1

continually worked over, are frequently cited, and have come to mark the parameters of a long-running debate about 'feminine writing'.

The main aim of this book is to try to put these two different versions of Cixous into some more active relation. Much of the argument about Cixous's 'theoretical' texts has suffered from inadequate attention to the context of their writing and to their relations to other elements of Cixous's work. Equally, much of the discussion of her work in France seems reluctant to take on the transformations in her writing as it has developed over the last twenty years, choosing instead either to place her definitively in the 1970s and within the problematic of 'writing the body', or to talk about her most recent work, with little attention to earlier texts and earlier literary and political commitments. To some extent, this problem is likely to arise in the discussion of any contemporary writer: critical categorization tends to replace complexity, and the urgency of her immediate writing tends to reshape understanding of her earlier texts. In Cixous's case, however, such partial accounts are particularly unhelpful, since it is precisely the modifications of her writing that allow us to assess the validity of her theoretical and critical claims, and to understand the shaping of her work in response to changing historical conditions.

Cixous's writing as a whole raises questions about the relations between politics and writing, the dimensions and implications of sexual difference, the possible interactions between philosophy and literature, and the tenability of an identity based on ethical, textual, and political difference from dominant social relations. It cannot be reduced to one 'position', or summed up by reference to one or two of her texts. Instead, it is important to examine the development of her critical and political ideas, as well as her writing practice, paying attention both to what is developed and what is discarded, in order to assess the significance and viability of her project as a whole.

Despite this commitment to seeing Cixous's work as a whole, however, it is with the better-known 'theoretical' Cixous that this book begins. Partly, the reason for this is strategic: a clarification of my readings of the texts with which readers are likely to be familiar may render my subsequent considerations of Cixous's critical, fictional, and dramatic texts more accessible. Secondly, although Cixous's theoretical writings exhibit many of the allusive, intertextual, and metaphoric qualities of her fiction, they are clearly written both for and within a recognizable set of theoretical debates. The meta-discursive illusion implicit in criticism is thus easier to sustain in relation to these texts: an illusion that seems important in an 'introductory' book. My reading of these theoretical writings aims to establish the parameters of Cixous's writing project, to establish the arguments she is making about writing and sexual difference, and to follow through the texture of these arguments in her discussions of literary and philosophical texts.

In the second chapter I look at Cixous as critic, analysing her readings of a range of writers, from James Joyce to Clarice Lispector. Although Cixous has been assimilated in both Britain and the USA as 'theorist', many of her theoretical positions are in fact developed from the close reading of a wide range of mostly European literary texts. A number of philosophers and theorists, particularly Freud and Derrida, have shaped her writing, but the most important source of her critical and theoretical positions seems to lie in the work of what amounts to an alternative canon of literary writers who challenge the dominant order of representation and of ethical values. Even when engaging explicitly with Freud, or Derrida, or Heidegger, she prefers to do so through the medium of literary texts, whose ambiguity and scandalousness she clearly values. In her readings of the works of Joyce, Hoffmann, Kleist, or Lispector, we can follow the development of her interests from a deconstructive commitment to the materiality of the signifier, through an exploration of subjectivity and sexuality, and towards the development of an alternative textual, political, and ethical economy which she describes as 'feminine'.

With the framework provided by her theoretical and critical writings, Cixous's fictional texts become more accessible. Equally, however, an exploration of her fictional writings clarifies much that she discusses in her theoretical and critical texts: particularly the priority of voice, the importance of lightness and 'flight', and the necessity of combining deconstructive and reconstructive techniques of writing. The sheer volume of Cixous's fictional writings precludes the possibility of any exhaustive treatment: a chronological gallop through her texts would, anyway, prove less than enlightening. Instead, I have focused on a relatively small number of her fictional texts, which seem to illuminate her writing project as it develops.[1] The non-availability of most of these texts in translation raises particular problems for the discussion of a writer who is so committed to the materiality of the signifier, and whose writing frequently plays on rhythms, verbal echoes, and puns, which are hard to render into English. My discussion of these texts has thus been forced towards a level of abstraction that does not always do justice to their linguistic specificity – a defect which I have tried to signal whenever it seems helpful to do so.

Cixous's fictional texts involve the intense working-over, and reworking, of a series of philosophical and textual problems, the constant exploitation of an intertext that includes, but exceeds, many of the works discussed by her in critical mode, a pushing of the limits of intelligibility to arrive at a style that is both dense and deceptively simple, a painful progression from an exploration of a violent and divided unconscious towards the assertion of an alternative form of subjectivity, and an interest in the intersubjective relations that underlie historical change. This move from exploration of the unconscious, towards an understanding of historical process which exceeds but does not exclude individual consciousness, is echoed in Cixous's work for the theatre.

The last chapter examines Cixous's theatrical texts, which have formed a major element of her writing in recent years. Here my aim is to explore the appeal of theatre as a form for Cixous, in a way that relates her dramatic writings to the rest of her work. Also, given that Cixous's identity in English Studies is so closely bound to her role as a theorist of 'feminine writing', I explore the implications of her move away from the exploration of individual feminine subjectivity, and towards an understanding of history as a struggle between competing economies, described as 'masculine' and 'feminine'. The movement of her writing towards the exploration of collective identities, and her extension of the theory of libidinal economies towards a model of social change, developments which have taken place in the context of the collective working practices of the Théâtre du Soleil, represent an exciting challenge to the narrowness of dominant versions of the 'literary', and offer the potential for a much more extensive use of her critical and theoretical ideas.

Overall, this book aims neither to praise Cixous nor to blame her. Instead, it recognizes the importance of her work for many of the issues that dominate contemporary literary and cultural studies, and attempts to put the ideas, techniques, and images found in her texts in their historical and philosophical contexts. If it also provokes in the reader a desire to explore more of her texts than the small number that have so far entered into theoretical debates, it will have served its purpose.

1

POLITICS AND WRITING

Despite the range of her fictional and dramatic texts, it is as a literary theorist that Hélène Cixous is best known in the English-speaking world.[1] Her essays on writing and sexual difference have been a crucial point of reference for feminist theorists and critics, and her insistence on the transformative and broadly political dimensions of writing has constituted an important challenge to the unfocused aestheticism of much of literary studies. In this chapter I will analyse the development of Cixous's ideas about the relations between writing and subjectivity, sexuality, and social change. Many of Cixous's arguments are developed in the context of close reading of literary texts, and I have thus returned to such texts where it seems helpful to do so, in order to identify the specificity of Cixous's readings.

Cixous's theorization of the politics of writing begins with an examination of the philosophical, political, and literary bases of patriarchy. In 'Sorties', an essay published in 1975, Cixous describes the set of hierarchical oppositions which, she argues, have structured western thought, and governed its political practice.[2] She cites oppositions such as 'culture/nature'; 'head/heart'; 'form/matter'; 'speaking/writing', and relates them to the opposition between 'man' and 'woman'. In each case, her critique of these rigid oppositions does not amount simply to an argument against dualism but rather to a political and philosophical rejection of the dialectical relation between each of these 'couples', which privileges one term of the opposition:

Theory of culture, theory of society, symbolic systems in general – art, religion, family, language – it is all developed while bringing the same schemes to light. And the movement whereby each opposition is set up to make sense is the movement through which the couple is destroyed. A universal battlefield. Each time, a war is let loose. Death is always at work.

('Sorties', p. 64)

Cixous does not invent these systems of oppositions: she reads them off a series of literary, mythical, and philosophical texts, finding their purest articulation in Hegel's *Phenomenology of Spirit*.[3] The danger, for Cixous, in such philosophical and social categories, lies in their absolute dependence on strategies of power and exclusion. Each couple is based on the repression of one of its terms, yet both terms are locked together in violent conflict. Without 'nature', 'culture' is meaningless, yet culture must continually struggle to negate nature, to dominate and control it, with obviously deadly results.

Cixous's earliest recognition of the effects of such hierarchical opposition took place in relation to the mechanisms of colonialism. Her experience of French rule in Algeria led her to identify a basic structure of power: the Arab population was both necessary to, and despised by, the French colonial power. Algeria, she argues, could never have been 'France': it was perceived as different and as dangerous. Yet the mechanisms of colonial rule necessitated its identification as 'French', as tied in a relation of dependence to the French state. Cixous thus identifies colonialism as a prime example of a dualist structure of unequal power, visited by the constant threat of violence. Both sides of the opposition are locked together, and the autonomy of one – in this case, Algeria – must constantly be negated by the other.

Such dialectical structures, Cixous argues, also dominate the formation of subjectivity, and thus of sexual difference. Cixous uses Hegel's 'master/slave' dialectic as the paradigm of a form of subjectivity which is both limited and destructive: 'a subjectivity that experiences itself only when it makes its law, its strength, its mastery felt' ('Sorties', p. 80). Here, subjectivity requires the recognition of an Other, from whom the individual differentiates him- or herself. Yet this recognition is experienced as threatening, and the Other is immediately repressed, so that the subject can return to the security and

7

certainty of self-knowledge: 'the dialectic, the subject's going out into the other *in order to come back* to itself, this entire process . . . is, in fact, what is commonly at work in our everyday banality' (p. 78).

This structure of subjectivity is related to the other 'couples' which Cixous has described: particularly 'man/woman'. Woman, within a patriarchal social and cultural formation, becomes figured, represented, as the Other, necessary to the constitution and recognition of identity, but always threatening to it. Sexual difference is thus locked into a structure of power, where difference, or otherness, is tolerated only when repressed. The movement of the Hegelian dialectic depends on an inequality of power between the two terms of opposition. Such inequality is then understood as the very basis of desire, that relation to the Other that is organized round the fear of castration, of loss and of otherness: 'It is *inequality* that triggers desire, as a desire – for appropriation. Without inequality, without struggle, there is inertia . . . ' (p. 79). Thus is constructed a desire that, Cixous argues, offers women the choice between 'castration' and 'decapitation': between internalization of a structure of desire based on loss, or deadly violence.[4]

Cixous's identification of this strategy of sexual differentiation is derived from the consideration of literary texts, of cultural representations. The story of the Sleeping Beauty seems to her typical of this structure of desire. The woman is represented as sleeping, as possessed of negative subjectivity, until her encounter with male subjectivity, with the kiss. The kiss gives her existence, but only within a mechanism that immediately subordinates her to the desire of 'the prince'. Cixous's reading of Joyce's *Ulysses* leads her to similar conclusions. Here the socio-cultural construction of women characters intersects with the structure of desire Cixous has described, to produce the figure of woman as confined to the marriage-bed, to childbirth, and to the death-bed: 'as if she were destined – in the distribution established by men . . . to be the nonsocial, nonpolitical, nonhuman half of the living structure' (p. 66).

It is important, here, to recognize the complexity of the relations that Cixous describes between the figure of 'woman', and women as historical subjects. Her argument depends on the importance of literary, philosophical, and mythical discourse to the formation of subjectivity. Such discourses do not exhaust the possibilities of subjectivity for individual women, but they do provide the structures in terms of which such subjectivity must be negotiated. The description of the construction of the figure of 'woman', and of its relation to mechanisms of desire, is thus of more than academic, or even philosophical, interest for women: it is the space in which they are placed by culture, and against which they must negotiate their own subjectivity.

Cixous describes her own historical recognition of this fact. Having first identified herself in terms of a common struggle, against colonialism and oppression, she comes to recognize that her gender makes such identification with a shared historical struggle problematic: 'No longer can I identify myself simply and directly with Samson or inhabit my glorious characters. My body is no longer innocently useful to my plans . . . I am a woman' (p. 74). She comes to see her own struggle as necessarily complicated by her gender, which cuts across available narratives of collective identity:

> 'We' struggle together, yes, but who is this 'we'? A man and beside him a thing, somebody . . . someone you are not conscious of, unless she effaces herself, acts the man, speaks and thinks that way. For a woman, what I am saying is trite. It has often been said. It is that experience that launched the front line of the feminist struggle in the U.S. and in France; discovering discrimination, the fundamental unconscious racism in places where, theoretically, it should not exist! A political irony . . . '
>
> (p. 75)

Cixous's strategies for transforming this dual, hierarchized structure of philosophical and political thought, and of cultural representations, are twofold. The first procedure amounts to a deconstructive reading, which is presented as a critique of the narrative of origins, of the 'Dawn of Phallocentrism'. This reading is intended to question the naturalness or inevitability of such structural hierarchies. The second involves an exploration of the subversive, and the political, possibilities of a writing practice that sets itself up in opposition to such cultural

9

categorization: a writing practice that Cixous describes as 'feminine'.

Cixous's representation of her project relies heavily on spatial metaphor. It thus amounts not simply to description, but to a writing practice that depends on allusion, metaphorization, and intertextual reference.[5] Cixous compares her attack on the origins of patriarchy to a mining of foundations: 'We are living in an age where the conceptual foundation of an ancient culture is in the process of being undermined by millions of a species of mole . . . never known before' (p. 65). The actions of this mole include the unearthing of the myths that sustain the logic of patriarchy, undoing their 'naturalness', and opening up the energies buried within them. This image of burial, and of possible mining and reworking, is reminiscent of Freud's observations on female sexuality. Freud comments on the surprise of his belated discovery of a period in the development of female sexuality that precedes the Oedipal in the following archaeological terms:

> Our insight into this early, pre-Oedipus phase in girls comes to us as a surprise, like the discovery in another field of the Minoan-Mycenean civilization behind the civilization of Greece.[6]

Cixous's archaeological researches lead her to an engagement with the mythical narratives surrounding the figure of Electra, through which she aims to provide a deconstructive reading of the 'Dawn of Phallocentrism', as she explores the possibilities of mining beneath the fixed structures of hierarchical dualities. She is also concerned with origins, with the recapturing of plurality in the face of teleology, and with 'the Law'.

The Law is understood as an abstract structure of prohibition and exclusion, and Cixous dramatizes what she sees as the dominant relation to the Law within patriarchy, through a reading of Kafka's short story, 'Before the Law'.[7] This story deals with a man who arrives before a doorway which gives access to the Law. When he arrives, the door is lying open, but the bearded doorkeeper convinces him that he cannot gain entry. Many years pass, as the man still stands in front of the door, apparently unable to enter. Eventually, however, 'before he dies, all his experiences in these long years gather themselves in his head to one point, a question he has not yet asked the doorkeeper'. He asks the doorkeeper why no-one else has come to the door seeking entry to the Law. The doorkeeper replies, 'No-one else could ever be admitted here, since this gate was made only for you. I am now going to shut it.' There had been no barrier, no exclusion, except in the man's own perception of his relation to the Law. The *that'* , knowledge of this fact, however, will die with him. Cixous *an example* uses this story as a compelling metaphor for women's relation *how she* to patriarchy: a social structure in which women submit to the *reads* Law, and die of it. Like Kafka's hero, women under patriarchy re-direct the power of which they are a source against themselves.

Cixous supports this analysis with a reading of the figure of Electra, as dramatized by Aeschylus and Sophocles.[8] She starts with what might seem an unhelpfully teleological narrative: 'The Dawn of Phallocentrism' ('Sorties', pp. 100–12). Cixous's analysis begins with a quotation from Freud's *Moses and Monotheism*:

> it came about that the matriarchal social order was succeeded by the patriarchal one – which, of course, involved a revolution in the juridical conditions that had so far prevailed. An echo of this revolution still seems to be audible in *The Oresteia* of Aeschylus. But this turning from the mother to the father points in addition to a victory of intellectuality over sensuality – that is, an advance in civilization, since maternity is proved by the evidence of the senses while paternity is a hypothesis, based on an inference and a premiss.[9]

Freud's argument about the development of patriarchy was not new: he was clearly indebted to the earlier theories of Bachofen, developed by Engels, which analysed the importance of this moment of transformation from matriarchy to patriarchy.[10] Both writers had argued for the existence of an earlier social formation based on the principles of matriarchy, with Engels relating the development of patriarchy explicitly to the growth of private property. We do not, of course, have to understand such analyses of matriarchy as literally, or historically, true: we can read them instead as a mythological positing of origins, or as narratives that seek to represent the development of patriarchy as progress, a movement from the sensual to the spiritual, and thus as emblematic of civilization.

11

Such narratives always risk, however, being read against the grain: that is to say, they can be read for the extent to which they make a structure other than patriarchy conceivable, and bring such a structure within the sphere of representation. We do not have to believe in the historical existence of matriarchy in order to make it sound like a good idea.

Cixous reads the *Oresteia* as a narrative of the formation of patriarchy. Seeing Orestes as placed at a turning point in history, Cixous focuses on the debate in the *Eumenides* over the relative claims of revenge for murder of a husband and murder of a mother. She draws attention to Apollo's ruling that 'the woman you call the mother of the child/is not the parent, just a nurse to the seed . . . /the *man* is the source of life', an account of reproduction that diminishes the gravity of matricide, and thus seems to license the development of patriarchal social relations (*Oresteia*, p. 260).

Cixous's interest in the *Oresteia*, and in the figure of Electra, does not, however, lie simply in the ways in which it dramatizes the origins of patriarchy: her aim is not to reprimand Aeschylus. Instead, she wants to read what is repressed in this myth of origins, to recapture the violence, the excess, and the death, that are an inescapable part of this putting-in-place of patriarchy; her project in reading the *Oresteia* is to challenge the seamless teleology of the narrative, and its apparent equation with progress. She explores the importance of deceit: the ways in which Orestes' pretended death is elaborately set up and developed, particularly in Sophocles' text:

> Under disguise and deviously hidden-hiding-disclosing in himself more than one nonhuman being, as being more than human, the shifty brother sets time ticking and explodes the feminine nucleus.
>
> ('Sorties', pp. 104–5)

This deceit is set alongside the disproportionate power given to the dead:

> The dead-father, Agamemnon (was he ever anything other than dead, except the day he was killed? Clytemnestra asks, but no-one hears the question), is in the strongest position: the position of death.
>
> (p. 104)

Cixous is fascinated by the active role of the dead, and by the different relations Electra and Orestes develop with their dead father. Electra calls to him to return, and asks him to take pity, but Orestes tries to blackmail him, saying that in return for intervention Orestes will keep his father alive. This relation between Orestes and his father, implicated as it is with blackmail and with death, is represented by Cixous as paradigmatic of the relations of patriarchy:

> In a certain way the father is always unknown. Coming from outside, he has to enter and give proof. Outsiders, absolutely other, strangers, ghosts, always capable of coming back. . . . Coming out of the earth to go back into the mother, into the palace, to reappropriate bodies and goods.
> That is what is called civilization.
> Progress, says Freud, whose logic thus expresses his self-interest in circular performances: 'Father, prefer me, so that feeling I am preferred, my self-confidence will grow so that I can call you "father" all the more loudly.'
> (pp. 111–12)

About this progress in 'spirituality' Cixous is scathing, focusing on its deathly, tomb-like location, and on its negation of much of the energy that has circulated around the figure of Electra. Electra is seen by Cixous as the leader of the phallocrats: her voice is the loudest in the demand for the death of her mother, Clytaemnestra. As such, Cixous contrasts her with the one last Great Woman, the one no man could 'keep', the inalterable Helen, or Hélène, whose departure 'left her land *chaos*, clanging shields/companions tramping, bronze prows, men in bronze' (*Oresteia*, p. 118). Yet Helen is banished from the text of the *Oresteia*, and only Electra remains ('orests', 'Sorties', p. 105) as the source of disruption. Arch-phallocrat, she is none the less disruptive in her excess. She generates a kind of 'Electricity', which lightens up the twilight of matriarchy. She manifests an 'infernal libido', and nothing can silence her voice; although, of course, Aeschylus silences her effectively by simply dropping her from the play with her final line containing the ironic demand 'hear us' (*Oresteia*, p. 200). Sophocles has Electra say, 'I will never cease my dirges and sorrowful laments' (*Electra*, p. 52), and this ceaselessness, Cixous argues,

13

takes her outside the circuit of exchange between father and son, outside the Law.

Electra occupies an ambiguous space, stretched between inside and outside, in relation to the family and the Law. She is at the threshold, but unlike Kafka's anonymous man she is not silent. She delivers 'a stream of cries, that won't run out, torment's spring that won't go dry' ('Sorties', p. 106). She is compared by Cixous to the effects of yellow amber when rubbed – that is, to Electricity. She interacts with the Chorus, Clytaemnestra, Chrysothemis, 'light bodies, attracted by magnetic Electra: an intense system of exchange, attraction, particle loss fed by Electra' (p. 106). Only Orestes is doggedly immune from the power of this electricity. Electra, Cixous argues, is both not woman and too much woman. She 'blazes the trail' to patriarchy, but in doing so generates energy and anger, which cannot easily be contained. Orestes recommends caution and silence, and struggles desperately to domesticate Electra.

The putting-in-place of patriarchy, which we can just as well understand as a metaphor for its continued operation, thus generates anger, excess, a voice that seems to escape control and instead goes underground, presumably to join the moles. The subjective and social 'splitting' this process involves is dramatized in the *Oresteia*, whose characters live their relation to the forms of patriarchy and matriarchy in their simultaneous presence:

> In this time of reversal everything is two-faced: one face still looks towards and old order; one face envisages the new power. The promised cutting works away on the body of each one.
>
> (p. 109)

Clytaemnestra is pulled to the past, haunted by dreams. Orestes lives a doubly double life: having died and not-died, and being doubled by Pylades, his 'silent shadow'. This image of subjectivity torn between two cultural orders, disputing possession of the body, is one that will recur frequently in 'Sorties' as Cixous theorizes the political potential of writing within her own history.

Her deconstructive reading of the *Oresteia* leads Cixous to challenge the notion that Aeschylus simply reinforces the hierarchical opposition 'feminine/masculine'.[11] After all, she

14

argues, the *Oresteia* is a mixed and undecided site, wherein active and passive forces clash, without being absolutely attributed to sexual difference. We can see examples of this in some of the unexpected attributions of 'femininity' and 'masculinity' in the text: Agamemnon complaining that in his homecoming he is treated like a woman; or Clytaemnestra becoming the bull who gores Agamemnon according to Cassandra's prophecy. None the less, Cixous argues, there is an attempt at closure in the text, and one which seeks to eradicate the echoes of Electra's voice. The patriarchal order is set in place ('patriarchy – politicaleconomy – sexualeconomy – it has all sorted itself out since they checkmated those great screeching females') and the electricity disappears from the text (p. 112).

In looking at this narrative of 'The Dawn of Phallocentrism', then, Cixous sought to open out the myth of Electra. She *myth* wanted to undermine the naturalness of the narrative, to set in play the violence, excess, splitting, and death that surround the moment of transformation from matriarchy to patriarchy, or rather that reverberate beneath the structures of patriarchal social relations. There are no feminist heroines in these texts of antiquity (except perhaps Hélène), and Electra is certainly not held up as the ideal of femininity. She is, however, seen as the site of articulation of much that is excluded from accounts of subjectivity that are based on a relation of power over the other, and also as a troubling complexity in the mythic origins of patriarchy.

Cixous's deconstructive reading of the origins of patriarchy shows great awareness of her own embeddedness in such narratives: their power is precisely the point of her analysis. Yet as feminist critique the reading is often frustrating, leading *her readings* to qualifications, tentative propositions, and ambiguous conclusions. The feeling of swimming in cultural mud is almost palpable, and it is with some relief that one turns to the other element of her strategy – the construction of an alternative practice of writing. As Cixous says: 'What I say has at least two sides and two aims: to break up, to destroy; and to foresee the unforeseeable, to project.'[12]

The first element of Cixous's theorization of the practice of feminine writing can be found in her discussion of alternative representations of sexual difference. She rejects the Freudian and Lacanian models, which she sees as condemning women to negativity in their privileging of the phallus as the organizing point of sexual identity and desire. Instead, she argues for the possibility of sustaining a bisexuality: not as a denial of sexual difference, but as a lived recognition of plurality, of the simultaneous presence of masculinity and femininity within an individual subject. Such bisexuality is open to all subjects who can escape from the subjective and social effects of the dominant structures of desire. Yet, Cixous argues, it is of particular relevance to women, since they have been the greatest victims of patriarchy:

> For historical reasons, at the present time it is woman who benefits from and opens up within this bisexuality beside itself, which does not annihilate differences but cheers them on, pursues them, adds more.
>
> ('Sorties', p. 85)

Cixous further argues that writing is a privileged space for the exploration of such non-hierarchically arranged bisexuality. Writing, she believes, can be the site of alternative economies: it is not obliged simply to reproduce the system. This argument is developed in the context of close readings of a series of texts, by Kleist, Shakespeare, and Genet, which she sees as dramatizing the limitations and violence of the *propre,* a term suggesting propriety, property, and homogeneity, which is generally translated as 'the selfsame'. She favours texts that are excessive in their characterization, that undermine the fixed categories of sexual identity. Thus, for example, Kleist's *Penthesilea*, the drama of an Amazon queen, attracts Cixous's attention.[13] She charts the unsettling of economies of war caused by the passionate love between Achilles and Penthesilea, and follows their relationship through to its catastrophic end: Penthesilea literally devours Achilles, consumes his flesh. Such violence, she argues, is both terrible and inevitable, revealing as it does the stakes invested in the economy of opposition and war.

From a commitment to the possibility of bisexuality, and its political importance for women, and a belief in the disruptive potential of writing, Cixous moves towards the production of a form of writing that would embody such bisexuality and operate in the interests of women. Her best-known statement of this project is contained in 'The Laugh of the Medusa'. This essay was published in 1975, in an issue of the journal *L'Arc* dedicated to Simone de Beauvoir. Much of the material in the essay is also contained in 'Sorties', but is presented in 'The Laugh of the Medusa' in more polemical fashion: most of the deconstructive argument is absent, leaving a seemingly less tentative, and perhaps less careful, but much more bracing version of her writing project. The rhetorical power of this essay is perhaps clearer in French, where a passage such as

> Nous, les précoces, nous les refoulées de la culture, les belles bouches barrées de bâillons, pollen, haleines coupées, nous les labyrinthes, les échelles, les espaces foulés; les volées, – nous sommes 'noires' *et* nous sommes belles.
>
> ('Le Rire', p. 41)

with its alliteration, its measured rhythm, its exploitation of the gendered nature of the French language, and its allusion to the 'Song of Songs' produces a more powerful effect than its English equivalent:

> We, the precocious, we the repressed of culture, our lovely mouths gagged with pollen, our wind knocked out of us, we the labyrinths, the ladders, the trampled spaces, the bevies – we are black and we are beautiful.
>
> ('Laugh', p. 248)

This essay has undoubtedly provoked strong reactions, and has been the focus of many of the frequent charges of 'essentialism': the claim that Cixous reduces women to an essence, specifically an anatomical essence, and thus negates the possibility of the very change which she seeks to promote.[14] It is thus worth considering the dimensions of her argument in some detail.

'The Laugh of the Medusa' begins by explaining that Cixous is trying to explore what feminine writing *'will do'* (p. 39). She is not trying to analyse what women have actually written, nor is she describing a writing technique that is natural to, or inevitable for, women. Her tentativeness is an important part of her argument, despite its polemic. In 'Sorties' Cixous is very careful to distinguish her analysis of sexuality from what she sees as the essentialism of Freud or Ernest Jones. Their theories, she says, rely on the visible: on the presence or absence

if Freud (penis envy + woman's lack) is based on visible
Cixous tries to locate sexual difference at level
of sexual pleasure, jouissance → realm of unknowable.

of the penis, or of an essential femininity. They are thus, she argues, 'voyeur's theories', tied to the metaphysics of presence ('Sorties', p. 82). Instead, Cixous tries to locate sexual difference at the level of sexual pleasure, of *jouissance*. To some extent, this is clearly a strategic move. It removes any possibility of identifying femininity and masculinity with the certainties of anatomical difference. It also places sexual difference in the realm of the unknowable. Apart from Tiresias, a figure to whom Cixous will return in *Le Nom d'Œdipe*, no-one, after all, is in a position to speak definitively about the dimensions of feminine and masculine *jouissance*. The insistence on libido as the location of sexual difference thus offers to Cixous the possibility of theorizing an alternative economy, of proposing an economy in which women, for historical and cultural reasons, have a particular investment, without allowing anyone the possibility of proving her wrong. Of course, it is also true that her theory cannot be confirmed, but since its function is strategic, intended to offer a political site of identification and shared struggle, this does not concern her unduly.

The location of sexual difference at the level of *jouissance*, however, does certainly return Cixous to the bodily; and that is where she wants to be:

> By writing her self, woman will return to the body which has been more than confiscated from her, which has been turned into the uncanny stranger on display – the ailing or dead figure, which so often turns out to be the nasty companion, the cause and location of inhibitions. Censor the body and you censor breath and speech at the same time.
>
> ('Laugh', p. 250)

She does not, however, equate the bodily with nature. She sees it as distinctly cultural, as caught up in representation, in language. As Barbara Freeman has argued:

> It is precisely the assumption of a non-textual body outside of language, of a linguistic domain which is not itself corporeal that Cixous's reformulation of mind-body relations in a feminine economy calls into question.[15]

Cixous argues that women's relations to their bodies are culturally inscribed, are related to the placing of women in the

18

sphere of the domestic, and to their lesser social possibilities for sublimation. She speculates on the possibility that the capacity to give birth may mean that women have a specific relation to their bodies, but is always aware of the dangers of being too dogmatic. Her most unambiguous statement of the power of sexual difference in 'Sorties' is followed by a painstaking articulation of the difficulties such a claim faces:

> But we must make no mistake: men and women are caught up in a web of age-old cultural determinations that are almost unanalyzable in their complexity. One can no more speak of 'woman' than of 'man' without being trapped within an ideological theater where the proliferation of representations, images, reflections, myths, identifications, transform, deform, constantly change everyone's Imaginary and invalidate in advance any conceptualization. . . . But we are still floundering – with a few exceptions – in Ancient History.
>
> (p. 83)

Cixous's return to the body is not an idiosyncratic move. She is writing at a moment when many philosophers and literary critics were returning to the bodily as the location of pleasure. The following extract:

> To write the body, neither the skin, nor the muscles, nor the bones, nor the nerves, but the rest: an awkward fibrous, shaggy, raveled thing, a clown's coat[16]

is not from Cixous but from Roland Barthes, in a text where he explores the bodily, as well as the discursive, constitution of his subjectivity. None the less, Cixous's commitment to the experience of writing as bodily has caused particular problems for feminist critics. Jane Gallop has written very interestingly about this problem: about the reluctance within feminist theory to accept 'the body as metaphor, a demand that metaphors of the body be read literally'.[17] Gallop attributes this reluctance to an association of the bodily with the natural, to a refusal to think through the extent to which the bodily, and experiences of sexuality, are cultural, are mediated by discourse: the extent to which we know and experience our bodies in relation to representation and narrative. To some extent, she is clearly correct, yet the worry is more substantial. Writing of the body,

19

we fear appropriation at the point where, historically, we have been most vulnerable, and where we have been so ruthlessly placed.

The most considered and careful analysis of the dilemmas of a return to the bodily, and particularly to images of maternity, is contained in Domna C. Stanton's 'Difference on Trial: A Critique of the Maternal Metaphor in Cixous, Irigaray and Kristeva'.[18] Stanton's argument shares many of the reservations of Alice Jardine's *Gynesis*, which explores the difficulties for feminist theorists of taking over the deconstructive project, with its privileging of the 'feminine', and its silence about women.[19] Stanton's reading is powerful, and refers in considerable detail to Cixous's fiction as well as to her theoretical writings. Her basic anxiety is that Cixous is returning to a metaphysics of identity and presence. The use of metaphor itself, she argues, alludes to an economy of similitude, rather than one of difference. Cixous's choice of the maternal as the strategic point of engagement with the politics of sexual difference, however, raises particular issues for Stanton, threatening as it does to return to the certainties of biology, and the 'naturalness' of motherhood.

To this dilemma there is, it seems, no answer, at least not within the political discourse of feminism. To evade the bodily is to reproduce a structure of oppression which has made of women's bodies their point of vulnerability and of guilt. To speak of the bodily risks a similar reproduction. At a fairly trite level, it is clear there is no escape. Yet this should not surprise us: one cannot simply walk out of patriarchy and shake off its effects. What Cixous tries to do is to subvert the discourse of patriarchy, to open it up to contradiction and to difference, while still retaining the possibility of shared recognition which would make a political movement of and for women possible. To what extent she succeeds cannot be answered in any totalizing or definitive way. For me, as I will argue in Chapter 3, some of her projections and mythical reworkings remain powerful, others produce unease. For others, such as Claudine Guégan Fisher or Verena Conley, the project as a whole is clearly both compelling and empowering.[20] What is, however, clear, is that Cixous cannot be accused of *naïveté*, or epistemological ignorance. She knows the dangers of essentialism – 'if one subscribes to . . . "anatomy is des-

20

tiny", one participates in condemning woman to death' ('Sorties', p. 82) – and recognizes both 'the mother' and 'the body'
as profoundly embedded in the cultural. What she does insist
on, however, is that that 'cultural' is organized differently for
men and women, and that a writing practice that will reformul-
ate the cultural will be of particular importance for women.

Cixous theorizes an alternative economy of femininity in
relation to the concept of 'the gift'. She describes two possible
attitudes to giving and to the intersubjective relations involved
in the gift: one, which she describes as 'masculine', is caught
up in the mechanisms of exchange, and will give only with a
certainty of immediate return. Exchange relations assume, by
definition, abstract equality, at least for the moment of
exchange, and thus exclude the recognition of difference. Cixous's alternative, or feminine, economy of giving seems to be
derived to some extent from the work of the anthropologist
Marcel Mauss, and from the development of Mauss's ideas by
Georges Bataille, and by Jacques Derrida.[21] Mauss's work was
concerned with forms of social exchange that preceded 'the
purely individual contract of the market place' (*The Gift*, p.
46). His research into the social relations of other societies,
and of earlier historical periods, led him to produce a theory
of 'the gift', as a form regulating intersubjective relations which
was both morally loaded and socially implicated. His text came
to be read as a form of critique against the individualism and
moral irresponsibility of abstract market relations. In adopting
the concept of 'the gift', in advocating a form of giving that is
not reducible to a single act of exchange, Cixous is not, as is
often suggested, adopting the discourse of idealism, but is
rather mobilizing a materialist account of social relations which
constitutes a critique of 'mass society'. This particular coincidence of modernist aesthetics and an opposition to the cultural
and political implications of 'mass culture' will be discussed
further in Chapter 2.

Having described the limitations of the masculine economy
of giving, and related this structure to the structure of dual
hierarchized oppositions and murderous subjectivity described
in 'Sorties', Cixous goes on to posit an alternative:

> Can one speak of another spending? Really, there is no
> 'free gift'. You never give something for nothing. But the

21

difference lies in the why and how of the gift, in the values that the gesture of giving affirms, causes to circulate; in the type of profit the giver draws from the gift and the use to which he or she puts it.

('Sorties', p. 87)

This different relation to giving is what Cixous sees as characteristic of an alternative, feminine, practice of writing. Such writing would not be afraid to go outside narrative structures, or to create subjectivities that are plural and shifting. It would not need to return to the security of fixed categories, of stable identity. It would *dépense*: a pun suggesting both the undoing of thought and a liberal spending of energies. It would be on the side of excess.

Cixous is very clear that feminine writing cannot be defined. She tries, particularly in 'The Laugh of the Medusa', to enact it. One characteristic which she does ascribe to it, however, is its proximity to voice. Partly, this is done in order to disrupt the opposition between speech and writing, by suggesting not only the presence of writing in speech, but also the potential presence of living speech in writing. It is also done in order to produce both individual and social change. Speaking, Cixous argues, is a powerfully transgressive action for women, whose bodies cannot be erased from their speech in the way that they have been from their writing. A woman speaking in public is seen first and foremost as a woman, not as a speaker. Finally, however, Cixous privileges speech because of its proximity to song, and thus to the unconscious: she wants to explore the associative logic of music over the linear logic of philosophical and literary discourse.

The specificity of feminine writing is also described in terms of spatial metaphor: 'If woman has always functioned "within" man's discourse . . . now it is time for her to displace this "within," explode it, overturn it, grab it, make it hers' ('Sorties', p. 95). Similarly, Cixous talks of feminine writing as happening in the 'between', in that space which is uncertain, dangerous in its refusal to ally itself with one side of an opposition. Stepping outside, negotiating the between, feminine writing is to carve out a new space of representation that will not fit into old grids.

Producing this form of writing is, for Cixous, a political act,

22

and is related to the desire to 'liberate the New Woman from the Old' ('Laugh', p. 248). The gesture that characterizes the relation of women to the cultural is one of flying and stealing [*voler*]. Women, Cixous argues, must steal what they need from the dominant culture, but then fly away with their cultural booty to the 'in between', where new images, new narratives, and new subjectivities can be created. *[magpie — take out of context]*

The call to writing for women is most marked in 'The Laugh of the Medusa'. Here Cixous speaks on behalf of women, and uses the pronoun 'we' with an ease and confidence that few of her other texts demonstrate. She knows, however, that many people will condemn her for this polemical strategy: 'Once more you'll say that all this smacks of "idealism," or what's worse, you'll splutter that I'm a "mystic"' ('Laugh', p. 262). She has, indeed, been accused of both. As we have seen, however, the argument of Cixous's early theoretical texts, is more complex, more careful, and more strategic, than such charges acknowledge.

Cixous began by theorizing the possibility of a model of sexual difference not based on exclusion or hierarchy, and relating this to a model of subjectivity based on openness to the Other rather than obliteration of the Other. She then argued for the possibility of understanding such sexual difference, not at the level of possession or absence of the penis/phallus, but at the level of *jouissance*. Such libidinal difference *[not penis but jouissance]* was then related to particular practices of writing, since writing was seen as a privileged space for transgression and transformation. The style of writing which Cixous describes as 'feminine' was then derived from a reading of a variety of literary texts, most of them written by men. Finally, in the last stage of her argument, Cixous introduced women, as historical subjects, arguing that women have had most to lose in patriarchy, and have most to gain from its defeat: 'It is in writing, from woman and towards woman . . . that woman will affirm woman somewhere other than in silence' ('Sorties', p. 93).

This focus on writing as a political strategy has very clear personal, and indeed biographical, significance for Cixous. This much is clear in reading Cixous's contribution to the volume entitled *La Venue à l'écriture*, which was published in 1977.[22] Cixous's article in this volume amounts to a biographical and theoretical explanation of her own relation to writing. The

23

volume also contains an article by Madeleine Gagnon, who tries to reclaim women's history through a reconsideration of the relations between sexuality and writing, and one by Annie Leclerc, who analyses problems of doubling, possession, and maternity through a reading of a painting by Vermeer. Echoing Cixous's project in 'Sorties', Leclerc again likens women's strategies in writing to the burrowing of a mole:

> Ce sont les fondations que nous minons peu à peu . . .
> nous les taupes innombrables, obscures et malicieuses.
> (*La Venue*, p. 150)

> [These are the foundations which we are mining little by little . . . we the moles who are beyond reckoning, dark and mischievous.]

Cixous's account of her relation to writing begins with her childhood, and in particular with the death of her father. She describes the ways in which writing seemed to offer the means to counteract the finality of death, a theme which also preoccupies her in *Prénoms de personne*, as well as in novels such as *Dedans* and *Tombe*. She also describes her entry into the texts and knowledges of the dominant culture, and the extent to which she felt they excluded her history and her experiences:

> Toutes les raisons pour lesquelles je croyais n'avoir pas le droit d'écrire, les bonnes et les moins bonnes, et les vraies fausses: – je n'ai pas de lieu d'où écrire. Aucun lieu légitime, ni terre, ni patrie, ni histoire à moi.
> (*Entre l'écriture*, p. 24)

> [All the reasons for which I believed that I did not have the right to write, good reasons, less good reasons, and those that were true and false: I had no place from which to write. No legitimate place, no land, no homeland, no history of my own.]

Despite her early passion for writing, then, what she experiences in her encounter with the dominant culture is loss and exclusion.

This sense of exclusion is related by Cixous to her identity as both woman and Jew: both tending to exclude her, to make her vulnerable to the Law. Her relation to language is marked by the complexity of her national identities. Her father was a Sephardic Jew, whose family came originally from Spain, but moved first to Morocco, and then to Algeria, where Cixous grew up and was educated within the French educational system. Her mother was an Ashkenazi Jew, whose family came from various regions of what was the Austro-Hungarian Empire. Cixous's 'mother tongue' was thus German, although the languages that surrounded her in Algeria were French and Arabic. She considers the effects of such linguistic diversity on her attitude to writing. For example, she stresses the musicality of German, and its profound bodily resonances for her – an observation that can perhaps be linked to her interest in the voice as part of writing. Similarly, she observes that she has always been fascinated by the resources of different languages, *(transl.)* and has approached each language delicately, in order to respect its specificity. The theoretical importance of this sense of linguistic distance and strangeness is stressed again by Cixous in a recent article where she writes that: 'the most important thing is that you never become too familiar and you never come to the point when you can hear it speak to you and you think you speak it'.[23] Such a detached, but emotionally charged, relation to language gives us an interesting insight into Cixous's capacity to exploit the power of the signifier to exceed any fixed meaning, and into her tendency to push the resources of language to their limits.

As 'La Venue à l'écriture' develops, what we experience is a sense of frustration, of urgency, and of anger. Again and again Cixous is confronted by the importance to her of writing, and by her incapacity to write. She is convinced that writing is the space of truth, and that truth is singular. Yet she experiences herself as heterogeneous, as made up of various identities, of many and varied desires, and concludes that she cannot be in the place of truth, or of writing. In reading this text we share Cixous's sense of frustration as she is repeatedly turned away from writing towards the restraint and the homogeneity in which she is culturally placed.

Eventually, however, Cixous describes her entry into writing: her first published volume of short stories came out when she was 30. The inner need to write is finally stronger than the pressures on her to silence. Women must have lost everything, have been driven to their limit, before they can risk the taboo of writing, Cixous argues. When they begin to write, they must remain in a critical relation to the languages and the narratives they inherit: they must invent new beginnings, remove themselves from the fixed categories and identities they have inhabited, explore the 'third body': which is neither the inside nor the outside, but the space between.[24]

Only through such exploration, Cixous argues, can women challenge the culturally produced category of 'woman'. The figure of 'woman' is a representation, projected by the Law, formed by exclusion and censure and by modes of thought based on hierarchy and opposition. In writing, Cixous argues, women can explore other identifications, other images, can rediscover some of what has been unexpressed, actively repressed. She suggests that a new form of shared identity is possible for women, formed not in relation to 'woman', but rather in terms of shared unconscious patterns and forms, which are the product of shared histories worked out across shared bodies.

'La Venue à l'écriture' ends on the positive invocation of an identity for women that might not be caught in the negativities of 'woman'. It has a happy ending: Cixous, after all, has clearly 'come to writing'. Yet this triumphant conclusion remains remarkably fleeting, and slippery. Cixous's final image of women's relations to writing is of fish swimming in water: reassuring, but hard to pin down.

Cixous's writings on writing, and on its political potential, are, then, a compound of the biographical, the strategic, and the theoretical. She offers her own history as part of her writing, as part of bringing other women to writing. She always reads this history in negotiation with theoretical and literary texts that seem to give it a more generalizing power: the power to explain, and to produce recognition, however tentative. She is aware of the dangers inherent in trying to speak or write as a woman, and aims to pick her way through the minefield of cultural stereotype, literary figure, and lived history. If she does not always succeed, we can perhaps more usefully reflect on the tendency of mines to explode, than rush to conclude that the field was never worth crossing.

Discussion of Cixous's writing in the 1970s would not be complete, however, without some reference to the institutional and political contexts in which her work was produced, and read, since these contexts clearly overdetermined responses to Cixous's work, both in France and in the United States. The French feminist movement of the 1970s was unhappily divided. The movement had grown very significantly since 1968: frustration and anger at the exclusion of women from the political structures of '68 led to a variety of opposing analyses of the appropriate strategies and theories to adopt. To some extent, the divisions seem very familiar to anyone involved in the history of feminist struggle in Britain or the USA. Radical feminists stressed the priority of women's oppression to any political analysis. Socialist feminists worked to integrate feminist struggle into the agenda of the Left. One particular movement, however, was fairly specific to the French political and intellectual scene – the group called 'Psychanalyse et Politique' (*Psych et Po*) who struggled to develop revolutionary theories of the oppression of women on the basis of psychoanalytic theory. The most prominent member of this group was Antoinette Fouque, and it was the group with which Cixous was most clearly identified.

Psych et Po set up the *des femmes* publishing house: an organization committed to the publishing of work by women, and in particular of contemporary work which seemed to fit within the parameters of 'feminine writing'. The bookshop *des femmes* was established in 1974, and the publishing house has continued to the present day. Despite its primary commitment to the publication of writing by women, *des femmes* does publish some work by men, and even appointed a man as commercial director in 1988.[25] The political strategy of *Psych et Po* was based on the necessity of challenging the unconscious structures of patriarchal oppression, and their policy was the by-now familiar one of working like 'moles' to disturb the dominant cultural and political order.[26] They were very hostile towards groups that described themselves as 'feminist', seeing such groups as reformist, and as working simply to gain access to, and to reproduce, the structures of masculine power.[27] They preferred to speak instead of the 'women's movement', and their outlook was resolutely internationalist, preferring to work on the possibilities of international support for women struggling against oppression, rather than to concentrate on domestic French politics. They were also committed to the importance of writing as a point of political struggle.

27

difference <—> *homogeneity*

The single greatest area of conflict between *Psych et Po* and other feminist groups lay in their attitude towards 'difference'. Feminists associated with the journal *Questions Féministes*, including Christine Delphy, Monique Wittig, and Simone de Beauvoir, believed that any discussion of 'difference' in relation to women was bound to reproduce existing hierarchies, and could only play out the existing stereotypes of 'woman's nature'. *Psych et Po* rejected this analysis, claiming that the fear of 'difference' within feminism led to reformism and homogeneity, instanced, for example, by the failure of US feminism to address the question of race.

unique of difference

This disagreement is profound, with clear implications for political strategy. It continues to provide one of the pivotal points of debates within feminist theory, as books like *The Future of Difference* make clear.[28] This theoretical difference, however, became overlaid with personal conflicts, displayed at conferences and in published texts and pamphlets. Tensions increased in the wake of legal actions initiated by *des femmes* against others involved in the women's movement, violent attacks on the bookshop *des femmes*, and the decision by *Psych et Po* to register 'MLF', the acronym of the Women's Liberation Movement, as their own trademark.[29]

The passion and anger that went into these debates and conflicts is now, more than ten years later, rather hard to recapture. Their usefulness for the feminist movement is certainly hard to determine. Yet they are important in the context of this book, since they affected the ways in which Cixous's work was read. Cixous published her fictional work exclusively with *des femmes* between 1976 and 1982, and has recently begun publishing with them again. This relationship with *des femmes* placed her inside the parameters of the struggle over difference, and tended to produce an attitude either of total loyalty or complete rejection – neither tending to aid discussion of the range of her work.

The other context which is important to the reception of Cixous's work is her association with the University of Paris VIII (Vincennes). This section of the University of Paris was set up after 1968, and Cixous was involved with it from the beginning. Vincennes was established in conscious opposition to existing institutions of higher education. It admitted students with 'non-standard' entrance qualifications, including many overseas students; it was interdisciplinary; it strove to diminish hierarchies between teacher and student; it rejected examinations in favour of continuous assessment.[30] It was also profoundly disliked by sections of the French establishment. It was at Vincennes that Cixous established the Centre d'Etudes Féminines, a centre committed to interdisciplinary research on the space of femininity within modernity. This development was explicitly attacked by the government, who took action in 1980 to prevent the awarding of higher degrees by the Centre. This action did not succeed in the long term, but it was an indication of the hostility with which Cixous's work was met by large sections of the political and literary establishment.[31]

Throughout the 1970s, Cixous continued to produce large numbers of fictional texts which set in play her ideas about femininity and writing, and explored subjectivity and intertextuality. This extended writing project will be discussed in Chapter 3. Her next important statement of the theoretical issues crucial to her work, however, appeared in the journal *Etudes Freudiennes* in 1983.[32] This took the form of an exploration of the figure of Tancredi, as represented by Torquato Tasso in *Jerusalem Delivered*, and by Rossini in the opera *Tancredi*.[33] Cixous used the figure of Tancredi as a means to dramatize the complexity of sexual difference, and as a linking point between textual, unconscious, and biographical explorations of such difference.

Cixous's attitude to Tasso's Tancredi has clearly changed since she wrote 'Sorties'. In 'Sorties' she compared Tasso unfavourably with Kleist, arguing that Penthesilea and Achilles represented a much more transgressive form of desire than that represented by the relationship between Tancredi and Clorinda: 'Tancredi passionately reuniting with Clorinda the moment he destroyed her aspect as a warrior. No *jouissance* then . . . ' (p. 118). But perhaps this shift should alert us to the dangers of claiming any 'definitiveness' for Cixous's readings of any given text. Cixous's readings are often related to a much wider project, aimed at opening up theoretical and political difficulties, rather than at summing up a text.

The figure of Tancredi with which Cixous engages is derived from two different sources. Tasso's poem, written in the late sixteenth century, deals with the struggles of the Crusader

29

army during the last few months before the conquest of Jerusalem in 1099. The Christian forces include Tancredi:

> With majesty his noble count'nance shone
>> High were his thoughts, his heart was bold in fight
>> . . . His fault was love.
>>> (Book I, Stanza 45)

Tancredi meets by chance, and falls in love with, a Muslim warrior, Clorinda:

> This lusty lady came from Persia late,
>> She with the Christians had encountered eft,
>> And in their flesh had opened many a gate
>> By which their youthful souls their bodies left.
>>> (Book II, Stanza 41)

During the course of a battle, Clorinda and Tancredi fight, unaware of each other's identity. Tancredi knocks off her helmet, recognizes her as the woman with whom he has fallen in love, and refuses to fight any more. Nine books later, they are once again locked in combat. By now we have heard Clorinda's life history, and have learned that she was actually born a Christian. Once again Tancredi is ignorant of his opponent's identity, and assumes he is fighting with 'some man of mickle might'. The struggle takes place at night, and continues with an intensity that lends to it an air of unreality, of dream. Eventually

> His sword into her bosom deep he drives,
>> And bath'd in lukewarm blood his iron cold
>>> (Book XII, Stanza 64)

and Clorinda dies, begging in her final moments for baptism. Only now does Tancredi realize what he has done. He

>> 'gan to tear and rend
> His hair, his face, his wounds: a purple flood
> Did from each side in rolling streams descend.
>>> (Stanza 83)

Tancredi expresses horror at what he has done, and proclaims his wish to die. He is then 'rescued' by a priest, who accuses him of having been in thrall to a non-Christian, and threatens him with damnation. Finally, Clorinda returns to Tancredi in a dream, thanks him for saving her soul, and talks passionately of her love for him.

This brief summary cannot do justice to the epic dimensions of Tasso's poem, nor to the power of the transgression represented by Tancredi and Clorinda's love. The fusion of passion and violence, the continual postponement of questions of identity, the enormity of the stakes between Christianity and Islam combine to give this element of Tasso's poem a resonance that disturbs the seeming neatness of its conclusion.

Rossini's Tancredi is also a warrior, and is also involved in fighting against Islam. The story is adapted from a tragedy by Voltaire. Tancredi's lover in this story is Amenaide, a woman who is wrongly suspected by her lover, and by all those around her, of being a traitor. Confusions of identity are, once more, important: a letter sent by Amenaide to Tancredi is assumed to have been sent to the leader of the enemy forces. Amenaide is condemned to death by her own father for her treachery, but saved by Tancredi who defends her honour in single combat, despite believing in her guilt. Tancredi is then fatally injured in the battle against the Saracens, but lives long enough to learn of Amenaide's innocence, and to be reunited with her.

The coincidence of names has led many critics to conclude that Rossini derived the plot of his opera from Tasso.[34] This is not, in fact, the case. The source is Voltaire's *Tancrède*, which is derived from a number of sources, including Ariosto. The confusion is not perhaps surprising. C.B. Beall notes:

> *Tancrède*, sujet qui vient de l'Arioste, mais dont l'esprit chevaleresque, la conception de l'amour et la scène de la mort présentent aussi des analogies avec le poème du Tasse.[35]

> [*Tancrède*, a subject derived from Ariosto, but one in which the spirit of chivalry, the conception of love, and the death scene are also to some extent analogous to elements of Tasso's poem.]

Cixous is not at all concerned, however, to claim that these two Tancredis are, in fact, 'the same'. Instead, she exploits the confusion surrounding their relations: 'there are several Tancredis, which is why I am having such a hard time trying

31

not to mislead us. . . . I am swimming between two Tancredis' ('Tancredi Continues', pp. 49 and 51). Her aim is to develop an argument about sexual difference and its representation across these Tancredis, across Clorinda and Amenaide.

Perhaps the most important fact about Rossini's hero is that the part is sung by a woman. It is a *travesti* role, originally, of course, destined for a *castrato*, but now providing a powerful and challenging role for singers of the calibre of Marilyn Horne.[36] Cixous's argument is closely related to the fact of operatic performance, to the presence of the woman's body and voice within the heroic man.

Cixous begins by stating her fascination with Tasso's Tancredi and Clorinda, who move outside the rigid categories of opposition and war, driven on by the power of their love. What interests her is '*the movement* of love', its inherent grace, which she describes as a 'gracious exchange' between pleasures (p. 37). This grace is set against the paralysis and limitations of fear. The abyss, the Law, is invented by our fear, and Cixous recommends the strategy of the acrobat, who leaps over the abyss with lightness and with grace.

When she turns to Rossini, Cixous tries to unravel the significance of the casting of Tancredi as a woman, a 'Tancreda'. Here, she argues, Rossini has perceived something essential to the character of Tancredi: his capacity to engage with the Other placing him firmly on the side of the feminine. This presence of the feminine in the masculine Cixous designates as 'Enigma', but also as her 'life work' (p. 39).

Cixous then moves towards a recreation of the power of *Tancredi* in performance: remembering the physical presence of two women, one in blue and one in white, singing of the power of their love. She is convinced that the force of that performance embodies an important secret about subjectivity and sexual difference, but is also tortured by her own inability to give form to this secret: 'I saw their secret. What I am telling of it is no more than light turned to dust' (p. 45).

The importance of this 'secret' leads her to reproduce it in the form of a dream. She describes her dream of a turquoise, luminous, beautiful, hanging above her, just out of reach: inside the turquoise is a pearl. The turquoise embodies the secret, but it cannot be grasped. Here then in this fusion of blue and white, this 'inside' and 'outside', this transparency and opacity, is a symbol of the complexity of sexual difference. The blue and white, echoing the costumes of Tancredi and Amenaide, can then be read as figures of masculinity and femininity, clearly different, but hard to open up, or to separate.

The dream imagery gives way to a description of Cixous's own desire for a relationship of love that would not be limited and paralysed by the rigid hierarchies of masculinity and femininity. In some powerfully lyrical passages, Cixous describes her love for another person, a person who has suffered from the distortions of gender identity, yet who remains plural: 'In any case she is not a woman. She is plural. Like all living beings who are sometimes invaded, sometimes populated, incarnated by others' (p. 40). 'She' also listens to *Tancredi*, which thus becomes something of a symbol of resistance to rigid categorization of sexual difference.

The point of Cixous's moving between text, performance, unconscious, and biography, lies in her unease about the capacity of words to hold out against the power of opposition. *Tancredi*, she argues, takes us to 'l'autre côté' [the other side] of hierarchies of sexual difference, another spatial metaphor which recurs in Cixous's texts, from her reading of Carroll's *Through the Looking-Glass* to her exploration of the Kingdom of the Dead in *La* (p. 39). The problem, however, is how to describe this other side without making it simply a mirror image of what we already have.

The dilemma Cixous faces is that 'the more I try to say, the more I feel I have wandered astray far from what, beneath appearances and secretly and obscurely, I am sure I have understood' (p. 41). She feels the pressure to produce formulae and solutions which are more dogmatic, more rigid, than her understanding of the 'movement' of sexual difference allows. She contemplates the possibility of giving up altogether on the project of trying to talk about sexual difference, about women and the economy of the feminine, since the pressure within this project to reproduce the dominant figures of the 'feminine' is so intense:

> But perhaps what is hardest and most necessary, is to positively forget these judges who make us answer their stupid summons stupidly, justify the non-justifiable,

speak silence, crush the music under the millstone of words, lie by swearing to tell only their truth, plead guilty to a lack of absence.

(pp. 49–50)

She talks once more of feeling oppressed by the 'word police', who demand fixity of meaning and of purpose. The word 'woman', she argues, carries such cultural weight, exists within so many historically embedded discourses, that by saying it again we are perhaps simply enclosing ourselves once more.

The solution to this problem cannot be simple: it persists with urgency throughout the whole of Cixous's writing. In the end, she admits, it cannot be run away from: 'nowadays there are so many clandestine massacres of women that a woman has to say "woman" a dozen times a day in order to protest' (p. 50). 'Tancredi Continues' is a contribution to the project of rethinking sexual difference. In it, Cixous tries to avoid the programmatic and the dogmatic, in favour of the allusive and the impressionistic. Her argument amounts to an insistence that we cannot determine the nature of 'femininity' once and for all, but can only hope, across a range of texts, to glimpse the possibility of a different economy of sexuality.

Cixous's continuing unease about the capacity of language to escape from cliché, and from the habitual, her frustration with its tendency towards reproduction of the status quo, has led her finally to consider the transgressive potential of painting as a form of representation. In an essay entitled 'Le dernier tableau ou le portrait de Dieu' [The Final Painting or the Portrait of God] Cixous considers the potential of painting as a site of representations that challenge the cultural-embeddedness of language.[37] The principal object of her analysis is Post-Impressionism. At first, what she detects in the paintings of Monet, or of Van Gogh, seems to be a kind of immediacy of visual and emotional impact. She describes her own desire to write like a painter: to communicate the full force of the instant, the colours and textures of the present moment. The same desire to express the intensity of the instantaneous is embodied in the concept of 'quasacles' ('quasi-miracle-instants') which Cixous describes, in a manner reminiscent of Woolf's 'moments of being' or Joyce's 'epiphanies', in her novel *With ou l'art de l'innocence* (p. 142). This intensity and

34

instantaneousness is, she suggests, something Clarice Lispector achieves, in a form of writing which has the force of a concentration of images, a series of paintings.

Cixous's attitude towards the painter at this point is one of jealousy: 'le peintre peut vous briser le cœur avec l'épiphanie d'une mer' [the painter can break your heart with the epiphany of a sea], while she herself can only name, or describe (p. 173). This consideration leads her to a reflection on the emotional power of language, which she sees as necessarily intersubjective. Thus she speculates on whether the very limitation of language, its inability to capture the visual force of the present, may not be its strength: its power depending absolutely on the active contribution of the reader.

The opposition at this point seems to be between the instantaneous plenitude of painting and the temporal intersubjectivity of writing. Like all such oppositions, however, this one is soon challenged. Cixous turns to a consideration of the phenomenon of repetition: a phenomenon important to the argument of *Prénoms de personne*. When she turns to the series of Monet's paintings of Rouen Cathedral, plenitude disappears, to be replaced by time and deferral:

> Voir la vérité de la cathédrale qui est vingt-six, et la noter, c'est-à-dire voir le temps. Peindre le temps. Peindre le mariage du temps et de la lumière.
>
> (p. 178)

[To see the truth of the cathedral that is twenty-six cathedrals, and to record it, that is to say to see time. To paint time. To paint the marriage of time and light.]

Painting then becomes a struggle against change and time, an attempt to capture the temporal within the instantaneous. The agonies of this process lead painters like Van Gogh to the necessity of speed in painting, as if quick execution could negate temporality, or even capture its form. Again Cixous sets up an opposition: between the slowness, the necessary deferral, of writing and the rapidity of visual representation.

What is at stake in this 'rapidity', for Cixous, is its power to force the painter outside the secure boundaries of the self, outside the categories of cultural expectation and cliché. Again the argument is one about 'grace': the audacious movement by the painter which refuses to acknowledge fear, in which the painter 'devient femme' [becomes woman] (p. 181). The possibility of such agility leads Cixous to a consideration of how it might be achieved in writing, how the false step and the false word could be avoided. Her object is the rediscovery of simplicity, a concept whose theoretical weight is developed through readings of Kleist, Heidegger, and Lispector.

Kleist introduces the possibility of rediscovering innocence through knowledge. Heidegger stresses the power of visual representation to communicate the being of Being: 'Van Gogh's painting is the disclosure of what the equipment, the pair of peasant shoes *is* in truth. This entity emerges into the unconcealedness of its being.'[38] Lispector provides the example of a form of writing that is painterly in its fidelity to the identity of individual things. The writer, Cixous argues, should imitate the painter in her refusal to stigmatize 'the ugly', in her capacity to see the possibility of significance and meaning in all objects.

The final turn against the 'plenitude' of representation comes when Cixous argues that the most important meaning of painting arises when all possibility of fixed meaning has been erased by repetition. Thus Monet's waterlilies, reappearing in so many different forms, point towards the infinite, the impossibility of closure in representation. The difficulty of painting points, however, towards the human importance of the attempt: the necessity to record the fact of impossibility, of repetition. In this project, Cixous states her alliance with the painter.

Yet one important difference remains. The painter deals with surfaces; Cixous wants to explore the inside, the underneath, the taste and the texture. When he was sent an apple as a gift, Monet could not bear to bite into it, and gave it away. This is an action Cixous rejects:

> Moi je l'aurais mangée. En cela je suis différente de ceux auxquels j'aimerais ressembler. Dans mon besoin de toucher la pomme sans la voir. De la connaître dans le noir. Avec mes doigts, avec mes lèvres, avec ma langue.
>
> (p. 200)

[For myself, I would have eaten it. In that way I am

36

different from those I would like to resemble. In my need to touch the apple without seeing it. To know it in darkness. With my fingers, with my lips, with my tongue and my language.]

Finally, then, in this dialogue between the writer and the painter, the writer holds her own. She asserts the possibility of transforming knowledge and experience through writing, and writes herself out of the trap of 'the habitual' which has threatened so many theorists of modernism.[39] The unease continues, however, about the complicity of writing with the hierarchical oppositions whose analysis was so important to 'Sorties'. It is perhaps for this reason that Cixous turns, in the 1980s, to theatre: a space that seems to embody the troubled relations between temporality, repetition, and immediacy which so fascinated her in painting.

2

STRATEGIES OF READING

Cixous's explorations of the transgressive, and the transformative, potential of language, take place in the context of a sustained engagement with other fictional and theoretical writers. Her readings of Kleist, or Joyce, or Lispector, are always linked to her desire to theorize the power of language to evade the habitual, to move beyond the hierarchies of dual opposition, and to challenge the deathly economy of intersubjectivity which she described in 'Sorties':

> Je demande à l'écriture ce que je demande au désir: qu'il n'ait aucun rapport avec la logique qui met le désir du côté de la possession, de l'acquisition, ou même de cette consommation–consumation qui, si glorieusement poussée à bout, lie (mé)connaissance avec la mort.
>
> (*Prénoms de personne*, p. 5)

> [What I ask of writing is what I ask of desire: that it should have no link with that logic which places desire on the side of possession, of acquisition, or even of that consumption–consummation which, so gloriously pushed to the limit, strikes up an (imaginary) relation with death.]

In an examination of Cixous's critical writings, then, it will be possible to see the development of her theoretical arguments in more concrete terms: from her early humanist commitment to literary creativity, through her later deconstructive engagement with subjectivity and the representation of sexual difference, to the positing of an alternative economy of representation.

This chapter will focus mainly on the writers Cixous has discussed at length in her three major critical works: *The Exile of James Joyce, Prénoms de personne* and *Entre l'écriture*.[1] These writers are James Joyce, E.T.A. Hoffmann, Heinrich Von Kleist, Edgar Allan Poe, Sigmund Freud, and Clarice Lispector, each of whom provides the site for a particular engagement with the politics of writing. In her readings of Joyce, Cixous moves from an exploration of the moral, intellectual, and political contexts of literary creation, towards an account of the constitutive power of language and its relations to the unconscious. The persistence of Joyce in Cixous's critical canon lends a certain status of 'typicality' to her readings of his texts, which allows us, through an analysis of these readings, to trace the shifting parameters of her wider critical project. Cixous's readings of Kleist, Hoffmann, and Freud are all related to the reformulation of subjectivity, on the basis of an understanding of the effectivity of the unconscious. Her interest in Poe seems to lie in the ways in which he explores the relations between writing and the structures of uncanniness and compulsion, which Freud had related to the death drive. When she turns to Lispector, however, Cixous's critical project is more explicitly related to the parameters of the 'feminine', as she analyses the libidinal economy that underlies Lispector's writing, discusses her representation of the experience of Being, and extols the scrupulous meanness of her prose. As in her more obviously 'theoretical' writings, what we will find in Cixous's critical readings is a realization of the necessity of a twofold strategy: a deconstructive engagement with existing forms of cultural representation, and an exploration of the possibility of an alternative economy of writing.

The number of writers who have significantly influenced Cixous is much larger than this brief summary suggests, and any account of the intertextual connections in Cixous's writing would have to involve reference to Kafka, Dostoevsky, Jean Genet, Osip Mandelshtam, Torquato Tasso, William Shakespeare, Lewis Carroll, Karen Blixen, and Marina Tsvetaeva, as well as to a series of mythological texts from both Egyptian and classical sources. Such connections have already emerged in the discussion of 'Sorties', but the power of this sort of intertextual collage will be discussed more fully when we come to examine Cixous's fictional texts. It is, however, clear that

Cixous is constantly involved in the constitution of a corpus of texts that engage with political and aesthetic problems related to her own aims. The literary forms which seem to hold most fascination for her, and from which she manages to produce the most productive readings, can be roughly divided into three groups: Early Modern (Tasso, and Shakespeare); German Romanticism (Kleist and Hoffmann); and Modernism (Joyce and Lispector). From these sets of texts she derives an understanding of the relations between subjectivity, textuality, and sexual difference, which is crucial to her own writing practice.

JAMES JOYCE

The first writer to whom Cixous gave sustained critical attention was James Joyce. He was the subject of her doctoral thesis, which was published in 1968 as *L'Exil de James Joyce* [The Exile of James Joyce], and he has continued to provide an important site for her theorization of writing, subjectivity, and sexual difference. *The Exile of James Joyce* is basically a study of the relations between Joyce's writing and his life. In it, Cixous reads Joyce's fictional texts in the context of letters and diaries, written by himself and by his brother Stanislaus. She explores, in particular, the development of Joyce's life, and his writing, from the position of *'non serviam'*, a refusal of all orthodoxies and a commitment to doubt as the only attitude consonant with reason; through an engagement with the Thomist concept of *'felix culpa'*, the belief that sin can be seen as positive, since it is necessarily linked to the possibility of redemption, or, in Joyce's case, to spiritual growth; and finally to an exploration of the constitutive nature of language in relation to reality. This development is linked to Joyce's changing formulation of the 'epiphany', from a quality inherent in the objects of everyday life, to a subjective experience of insight and intensity. Cixous bases her analysis on the concept of 'exile', understood as flight, as a position of critical realism, and finally as the exile of the soul which provides the energy and the structures of Joyce's writing. This reading makes of Joyce's play, *Exiles*, a crucial text, both in relation to Joyce's biography and in terms of his representation of subjectivity. Here, in this play about triangular erotic relations, Joyce explores 'the voluntary

splitting of the self' which will be so important to the representation of Stephen Dedalus and Leopold Bloom in *Ulysses* (*Exile*,
p. 561). The play is thus seen as constituting a kind of 'epistemological break' within the canon of Joyce's writing, and as
allowing in *Ulysses* and *Finnegans Wake* the full exploration of
the relations between subjectivity and language hinted at in
Dubliners and in *A Portrait of the Artist as a Young Man*.

Cixous's conviction that Joyce wrote his life, rather than
living it, leads her to read biography and literary text together,
using in particular the figures of Stephen Hero and Stephen
Dedalus as a means to open out Joyce's aesthetic and ethical
commitments (*L'Exil*, p. 10). The drawback of this procedure
is that it leads to a dissipation of Cixous's own critical voice,
which often seems to be swamped by the plethora of texts
with which she is engaging. This dilution seems particularly
disabling when Cixous seeks to analyse the sexual politics
implicit in Joyce's aesthetic practice.

At one level, Cixous clearly wishes to take issue with Joyce's
construction of 'The Artist as Cannibal' (her chapter 6), and
she criticizes the way in which 'he wiped out from his artistic
memory the mother's love and transformed her into a figure
standing for the Church and death' (*Exile*, p. 119) or the way
in which Joyce used the figure of universal woman: 'he can
make use of her, tranquilly assured that she has no inner self
or personality or individual opinions which might hinder this
utilisation' (*Exile*, p. 486). Such punctual criticism is, however,
marginalized by the overall conception of the book. For her
account of the people who surrounded him, Cixous is largely
reliant on Joyce's own texts. This seems to make it very difficult
for her to challenge the terms in which he articulates his aesthetic and personal project. Thus Cixous reproduces Joyce's
version of the modern woman, as represented by the figure
of Emma Cleary in *Stephen Hero*:

> she takes pleasure in teasing and in keeping the young
> men at a distance; she feeds on incense and compliments
> with double meanings, flattery, tea and little cakes . . .
> she is, in short, a fashionable young woman who prides
> herself on being patriotic, disguising her desire to be
> courted as a desire to share in progressive idealism with
> the young man
>
> (*Exile*, p. 491)

41

with such conviction that it reads like endorsement. The same is true of the ways in which Cixous represents the women in Joyce's life, suggesting that both Joyce's mother and his wife were actually rather powerful, precisely because of their status as victim: 'Her passivity and silence are the weapons of her power' (*Exile*, p. 28). Such a claim that oppression and passivity constitute a form of power is certainly a familiar one, but none the more comfortable for that.

The difficulty lies not just in the fact that Cixous accepts relatively uncritically Joyce's representations of women, but rather in the teleological structure of developing creativity that Cixous reads into Joyce's life. All of the tensions, conflicts, and contradictions of his life are read as a necessary part of the development of Joyce the artist. To take issue with any of these, or with the terms in which they are represented, would thus amount to taking issue with the status of Joyce as artist, something which, in this text, Cixous is not really prepared to do.

The Exile of James Joyce ends with a consideration of Joyce's innovations in the representation of the relation between language and subjectivity. These include his consideration in *Dubliners* of the physical power of words,

> every night as I gazed up at the window I said softly to myself the word paralysis. It had always sounded strangely in my ears like the word gnomon in the Euclid and the word simony in the catechism. But now it sounded to me like the name of some maleficent and sinful being. It filled me with fear, and yet I longed to be nearer to it and to look upon its deadly work;
>
> (p. 7)

his dissociation of signifier and signified, through unconscious association or pun; and his challenge to language as a net, limiting rather than reflecting experience of the real. These are the aspects of Joyce's writing that occupy Cixous in the series of texts dedicated to him in *Prénoms de personne*.[2] Cixous here begins to explore Joyce's writing in a more deconstructive manner, stressing the ways in which he challenges readability, resists narrative structure, and interrogates the processes of naming. Cixous describes Joyce's writing practice as amounting to a form of 'permanent revolution' in its resistance to codification, to imperialism, to familialism, and to all forms of propriety (pp. 233–4). She analyses the way in which narrative point of view is multiplied, unsettled, undermined, particularly in the 'Circe' chapter of *Ulysses*, where Joyce dramatizes the collision of all of the subjectivities represented in the text, both living and dead, in a brothel scene involving erotic fantasy and sex change. Cixous relates Joyce's texts to the German tradition of *Bildungsroman*, the novel of apprenticeship in life, of learning, of developing subjectivity. Having begun with a desire to unify the fictional subject in *Portrait*, 'le désir d'un *Portrait* rabat toutes les possibilités, dans le cadre d'une actualisation d'un propre' [the desire of a *Portrait* closes off all possibilities, within the framework of a realization of the self-same] (p. 261); Joyce then moves towards an understanding of the necessary breach within the self, and to a representation of the complex of conscious and unconscious processes which constitute that self.

Already, in *Portrait*, Joyce had explored the relation between naming and fixity, but in *Finnegans Wake*, Cixous argues, he dramatizes the refusal of such naming, the journey of 'Personne' (p. 262). This is accomplished through the audacity of his linguistic experimentation, which divorces language from its seemingly automatic relation with the real, and opens it up to multiple meanings, and to unconscious thought. Both the continuities and the differences between these two texts can be seen in the following passages:

> The face and the voice went away. Sorry because he was afraid. Afraid that it was some disease. Canker was a disease of plants and cancer one of animals: or another different. That was a long time ago then out on the playgrounds in the evening light, creeping from point to point on the fringe of his line, a heavy bird flying low through the grey light. Leicester Abbey lit up. Wolsey died there. The abbots buried him themselves.
>
> (*Portrait*, p. 22)

> riverrun, past Eve and Adam's, from swerve of shore to bend of bay, brings us by a commodius vicus of recirculation back to Howth Castle and Environs.

Sir Tristam, violer d'amores, fr'over the short sea, had passencore rearrived from North Armorica on this side the scraggy isthmus of Europe Minor to wielderfight his penisolate war.

(*Finnegans Wake*, p. 3)

Both these passages use punning, multiple meaning, and shifting point of view, yet *Finnegans Wake* is more excessive in its project of forcing the reader into an active relation with the text, and breaking up the semantic and syntactic closure of language. For Cixous, the implications of such writing practices exceed the literary or the philosophical, 'Que la critique du logocentrisme soit inséparable d'une mise en question du phallocentrisme, Joyce le sait immédiatement' [Joyce knows immediately that the critique of logocentrism is inseparable from a challenge to phallocentrism] (*Prénoms*, p. 236): a recognizably Derridean position, which Cixous was to explore at greater length in 'Sorties'. At this stage, however, Cixous is setting the agenda for much of her subsequent work. The focus is no longer on Joyce the Artist, but rather on Joyce the writer: his texts are valued as the point of intersection between fiction and theory, between art and revolution (*Prénoms*, p. 237).

In later writings on Joyce, published in *Entre l'écriture*, Cixous focuses more intently both on *Finnegans Wake* and on questions of sexual difference.[3] Her points of entry to Joyce's texts include an examination of his linguistic deconstruction of the Law, as well as an assessment of the ways in which the discourses of history and myth pervade his texts ('Freincipe'). The most distinctive reading, however, is of pp. 164 ff. of *Finnegans Wake* where, 'looking wantingly around our undistributed middle between males we feel we must waistfully woent a female to focus and on this stage there pleasantly appears the cowrymaid M.'. Cixous uses this section as the basis for an exploration of the disturbance caused to patriarchal thought by the representation of female subjectivity. The entry of M. clearly unsettles the narrative voice: at first it expresses sexual desire ('*I cream for thee, Sweet Margareen*'); then an effort is made to contain M. within a frame of exactly mathematical proportions ('*The Very Picture of a Needlesswoman*'). There then follows an attempt to relate her to everywoman ('totamulier'),

44

a jealous diatribe, and an increasingly disorientated and desperate conclusion where the text comes very close to falling apart ('The word is my Wife, to exponse and expound, to vend and to velnerate, and may the curlews crown our nuptias! Till Breath us depart!').

The discussion of this passage marks an important departure for Cixous. In earlier texts, her attitude towards Joyce's 'universal' female characters, such as Molly Bloom, or Gretta Conroy, was fairly uncritical. She seemed to valorize the fact of their being given a space, rather than to question the very constitution of such a universality:

> Dans *les Morts*, la femme singulière, universelle fait son apparition première, définitive. Gretta . . . [accède] à la position souveraine du Sujet, celle dont la littérature n'avait supporté jusque-là l'irruption, avec l'opaque puissance de l'Inconscient, son innocence cruelle, sa force germinative, sa grâce.
>
> (*Prénoms*, p. 289)

> [In *The Dead*, the singular, universal woman makes her first and definitive appearance. Gretta . . . reaches the sovereign position of subject, the position whose violent entry literature had never been able to tolerate up to that point, with the impenetrable power of the Unconscious, its germinating force, its grace.]

In 'La Missexualité', however, Cixous is much more aware of the ways in which such figures of the feminine can be complicit with patriarchal thought. M. is 'l'étrangère sans laquelle le propre n'aurait pas de milieu en lequel s'extérioriser pour revenir à soi' [The strange woman, without whom the self-same would have no medium in which to externalize himself, in order to come back again to his own self] (p. 79). What fascinates Cixous is not the 'truth' of M., but rather the effect her presence has on the writing, and on the figure of Shaun/Jones. Jones's attempt at mastery over the wayward figure of M. fails: his picture of a needless woman cannot be drawn.[4] Cixous is not celebrating the figure of M., but rather analysing the ways in which her 'misstery' resists attempts at categorization. The object of analysis is not women, but rather their representation, and Cixous values the way in which Joyce lays out the structures of patriarchal thought and allows them, if only briefly, to self-destruct.

FREUD, HOFFMANN, KLEIST

'Self-destruction' also turns out to be an important theme in Cixous's readings of the work of Hoffmann and Kleist: readings which explore the relations between language and subjectivity, and refer the power of Hoffmann and Kleist's texts to the structures of repetition explored in Freud's essay on 'The Uncanny'.[5] Cixous's interest is in forms of writing that disturb the notion of individual subjectivity as unified and stable, and explode the boundaries of the self. Using the ambiguity of the word 'personne', which suggests both a person or personality, and also its negation, a 'nobody', Cixous explores questions of negation, identity, and naming, in their relation to the unconscious. Cixous is aware that such a deconstructive questioning of the stability of the individual subject is not without precedent: what interests her, however, is the extent to which she can find the beginnings of such explorations in texts written over one hundred years before the advent of 'modernism'.

Cixous's reading of Hoffmann is developed in relation to Freud's essay on the 'uncanny': a text where Freud tries to theorize the role of the unconscious in response to unsettling phenomena such as coincidences, doubles, repetitions, or fits. Freud's starting point is a text by the psychologist Jentsch, who had examined the question of 'uncanniness' and related it to intellectual uncertainty, particularly uncertainty about the attribution of consciousness to an object such as a puppet, or to a person in the grasp of an epileptic fit.[6] Freud finds this explanation unsatisfactory, and prefers instead to explore the ways in which particular manifestations of the uncanny seem to be related to unconscious wishes or fears. He begins by exploring the complex of meanings surrounding the uncanny (*unheimlich*) and its opposite, *heimlich*. The word *heimlich*, Freud argues, has two sets of meanings, one associated with the familiar and the homely, the other with something that is hidden, or out of sight. *Unheimlich* seems to trade on both these meanings, suggesting both something strange and something that should be hidden but has now come into sight. It thus suggests both the unfamiliar, and that which was known but has been hidden:

> Heimlich is a word the meaning of which develops in the direction of ambivalence, until it finally coincides with its opposite, *unheimlich*.

(p. 226)

Finding no resolution in this sort of linguistic analysis, Freud turns instead to one of the texts analysed by Jentsch, Hoffmann's 'The Sandman'. 'The Sandman' tells the story of a young man's disastrous infatuation with Olympia, a young woman who turns out to be a very cleverly constructed puppet. Nathaniel's psychic disturbances go back to his childhood, when he conceived a morbid terror of a character called Coppelius, a man who visited his father and apparently collaborated with him in alchemical experiments, but whom Nathaniel conceived of as the legendary 'Sandman', who visited naughty children and stole their eyes. Later in life, Nathaniel is convinced that he has once more found Coppelius, in the figure of a man called Coppola, who tries to sell him 'eyes', an offer apparently referring to the spectacles and telescopes in which he deals. When he looks through one of the telescopes, Nathaniel at last sees 'Olympia's beautiful face', and, as he watches it, it becomes increasingly animated. Nathaniel is besotted: he forgets about his love for the virtuous Clara, and pursues Olympia with all his energies. The fact that Olympia never speaks does not trouble him, nor does the fact that her eyes seem only to reflect his own. Eventually, and traumatically, Nathaniel discovers the truth about Olympia: a truth which causes great social anxiety as husbands start to ask their wives to speak, to exhibit imperfection, lest they too should turn out to be dolls. Clara takes Nathaniel back, and it seems that he will be reappropriated by the familial and the 'normal'. However, at the end of the story, Coppola reappears, apparently in order to drive Nathaniel to his ruin: Nathaniel plunges to his death from a high tower.

Jentsch's analysis of this story focused on the figure of Olympia, and the intellectual uncertainty that surrounds her status for most of the story. Freud, however, has little to say about Olympia, and turns instead to Nathaniel. The notion of something both dreaded and familiar strikes Freud as an appropriate metaphor for the unconscious, and it is in Nathaniel's unconscious that Freud looks for the site of the uncanny. Freud reads Nathaniel's obsession with eyes as a displaced fear of castration, and sees the 'Sandman' who threatens to steal eyes as a version of the father. Olympia, too, in this reading becomes a figure in the Oedipal relation between father and son, understood as 'a materialization of Nathaniel's feminine attitude towards his father in his infancy' (p. 232, n.). Nathaniel is described by Freud as a man fixated upon his father by a castration complex, who is incapable of loving a woman.

The difficulty with this reading is that its neatness seems to remove the very 'uncanniness' which Freud wanted to analyse. He admits as much, and refers to the necessity for further consideration of the ways in which fictionality complicates the structures he has identified. He refers such an enquiry to the realms of aesthetics, but does not really undertake it, beyond remarking that it is something to do with the disruption caused by the claim by a writer 'to move in the world of common reality' (p. 250). For Cixous, however, it is precisely the relations between fictionality and the uncanny that are important. The idea that fiction might have a privileged relation to exploration of the unconscious is a useful one for a writer who looks to literary texts as the site of oppositional versions of subjectivity. Thus Cixous extends, and takes issue with, both Freud's analysis of the uncanny and his reading of 'The Sandman'.[7]

Cixous argues that the unease which Freud exhibits over his discovery of the instability of meanings surrounding the *unheimlich* leads him to a reductive reading of 'The Sandman' – a reading that effectively excludes Olympia. Cixous returns to Jentsch's concept of 'intellectual uncertainty' as a crucial component of 'The Sandman'. For Cixous, however, the uncertainty does not relate simply to the question of Olympia's status as 'living doll'. Rather, the very possibility of confusion between a human being and a doll opens out the question of the simulacrum and its social effects. In a reading that refers explicitly to Derrida's 'La double séance' Cixous considers the ways in which the possibility of a perfect copy threatens the economy of representation, destroying the completeness and uniqueness on which it depends.[8] She thus finds a way of reading 'The Sandman', and its uncanniness, which returns to the figure of Olympia, and focuses on the extent to which she can be understood as a metaphor for a disorder in the economy of representation.

Overall, however, Cixous does not really find this reading adequate to the power of Hoffmann's text, and, like Freud, she returns to Nathaniel. Cixous stresses the importance of Olympia as a figure of femininity, believing this to be the source of her disruptive power and the reason for Freud's evasions:

> Un peu trop de femme dans l'automate, un peu trop d'automate dans la femme, la même pénible menace de l'hétérogène inquiète'.
>
> ('Les noms du pire', p. 52)

> [A little too much woman in the automaton, a little too much automaton in the woman, the same painful threat of heterogeneity disturbs.]

The distinctiveness of Nathaniel, Cixous argues, lies in his openness to Olympia. Turning away from the repressive rationality of Clara, Nathaniel moves towards a relationship which is detached from the couple 'reality/fiction'. He is on the side of change, of risk, of movement outside the social and beyond the human. His desire produces the disordered narrative, the strangeness, in this text where love and death battle for precedence. It is Nathaniel who leads us to that uncanny place where desire is produced in fiction.

It is hard not to agree that the force of Nathaniel's desire constitutes part of the fascination of this story. The disruptive potential of his desire is, however, open to question. The very ease with which Freud managed to turn this into a story without Olympia suggests that the femininity Olympia represents can be contained within patriarchal models. Olympia was, after all, manufactured to respond to the need for mirroring, for a passive Other. Nathaniel's self-destructive obsession with Olympia and with Coppelius does disrupt the narrative structure of this story, breaking down the possibility of linear exposition and fracturing the narrative voice, and his choices do indeed negate the familial as a solution to such insistent desire. However, the story finally hangs on a crucial opposition which is nowhere challenged, not even by Cixous: the opposition between the repressive function of Clara and the licence of Olympia. This is the opposition that makes of Nathaniel a hero, by perpetuating the representation of woman as either virgin or whore.

Cixous's reading of Kleist's essay on the 'Marionette Theatre' is a more focused, and a more productive, interrogation of questions of fictionality and subjectivity.[9] Kleist's brief essay is a dialogue between a narrator and a dancer, about the relations between consciousness and beauty or grace. The dancer argues that marionettes have a lot to teach dancers about grace of movement. Marionettes move according to mechanical laws, unencumbered by consciousness. They are free from the affectation that accompanies self-consciousness, and simply move in response to the manipulation of their centres of gravity by the puppeteer. In the human dancer, however, knowledge gets in the way, and moves the creative soul away from the point of gravity, thus causing imperfections of movement and lack of grace. Similarly, it is argued, the perfection of movement of a young man can be destroyed by his catching a glimpse of himself in the mirror, becoming aware of himself as beautiful. Both these arguments amount to a radically anti-humanist aesthetic; stressing beauty as a formal property, rather than a moral or intellectual category. The effects of human consciousness are similarly criticized in the final example discussed in Kleist's essay, that of a fighting bear. The conclusion drawn is that an animal is a more successful fighter, because he can form an imaginative relationship with his opponent, while the human being remains trapped within his self-conscious fantasies of domination. This point is very similar to the arguments made by Poe in his consideration of the basis of analytic thought.[10]

Kleist's text, does not, however, conclude with anti-humanism. Both alternative knowledges and transcendence of the dichotomy between infinite knowledge and total ignorance (God and doll) are explored in a complex image of the effect on geometrical figures of passing through infinity. Eating again at the tree of knowledge, passing through infinity in order to re-enter the world from the other side, may lead us back to innocence, and thus free us from the burdens of consciousness. It must be said, however, that Kleist's argument here strains the limits of the conceivable, and we are left concluding that it would certainly be easier to achieve grace were we either Gods or dolls.

Cixous observes first of all the ways in which Kleist's text embodies his argument. The autonomy of the marionette, who produces meaning and beauty from a system of movement, rather than as an expression of individual consciousness, is repeated in the autonomy of the text, which produces meanings from a system of signification, rather than simply expressing a unified consciousness. Cixous identifies the dancer's argument as materialist, yet insists that it does not remove the question of grace, or of creativity. 'Human nature' as a stable determinant of aesthetic beauty is challenged, but the importance of theorizing the power of the aesthetic remains:

> 'Et si la fétichisation ne serait pas un exercice tel qu'il dissoudrait un moi illusoire. Au lieu du moi gouvernant, c'est la réalité affective, faite d'un mélange du corps du sujet avec plusieurs autres corps également affectifs, qui passerait par tel organe, muscle, ou articulation qu'elle *obsèderait*, [*sic*] qu'elle posséderait physiquement'.
>
> ('Les marionnettes', p. 137)

> [And whether fetishization is not an exercise capable of dissolving an illusory ego; homing in on, physically possessing, not the ruling ego, but affective reality, made up of a mingling of the subject's body with several other equally affective bodies, which operates through a given organ, muscle, or joint.]

Kleist's essay, then, leads Cixous to consider the difficulties of developing a non-reductive, materialist aesthetics. She remains unconvinced by Kleist's concluding image of the possibility of transcendence, pointing out that this image closes off the complexity of the issues suggested by the essay. The story of the young man and the mirror leads her to argue that the knowledge of sexual difference may turn out to be a particularly disabling sort of knowledge; this dramatized 'mirror stage' showing the relations between recognition of sexuality and desire, and a destructive self-consciousness. Finally, however, Cixous pins her hopes on the bear, a figure who will return in *L'Indiade*. What the fighting bear exhibits is neither ignorance nor divine knowledge, but rather a different sort of knowledge. This knowledge involves intersubjectivity – consideration of self in relation to another. Thus Cixous is happy to reject the stability of individual identity, and the possibility of a humanist basis for aesthetics, in return for a materialist aesthetic based on the possibility of intersubjectivity, of a creative relation with the Other.

EDGAR ALLAN POE

In writing about Poe, Cixous is joining the significant number of critics who have been interested in Poe for the ways in which his writing exceeds expectations of the novelistic, explores structures of subjectivity, and seems to foreshadow many of the formal and thematic concerns of modernism. T. S. Eliot, for example, in *From Poe to Valéry* (1948), argued that Poe was 'a kind of displaced European' whose poetry, with its interest in immediacy, in the material texture of words, provided an important source for French symbolist poetry (p. 9).

This perception of an American writer of the early nineteenth century as having a place in the history of European writing owes much to the influence of Baudelaire. Baudelaire translated Poe into French, as well as providing critical and biographical introductions to his work. Baudelaire was interested in Poe as one of a number of philosophical novelists: a select category including Hoffmann and Goethe. Such writers were distinguished by their interest in the minute workings of the human soul, and in the supernatural, but also by what Baudelaire referred to as their 'philosophical mania'. By this he meant that they tended towards the construction of more and more esoteric philosophical systems, to which they were committed to the point of excess. Baudelaire clearly admires such writers for their spirit of *chercherie*, a primitive searching into the roots of human behaviour, and also for the ways in which they disturb the closure of philosophical systems, with sudden breaches and assaults of imaginative energy.[11]

The main source of Baudelaire's interest in Poe, however, lay in the extent to which he could be understood as a figure of revolt against the values and the norms of bourgeois life. Poe was seen by Baudelaire as heroic in his capacity to live as an outcast, to challenge the 'pitiless dictator' that is public

opinion in a democratic society.[12] Baudelaire's own increasing
alienation from developments in French culture and politics of
the 1850s had led him to reject the progressive pretensions of
the bourgeoisie, and to pin his hopes on the aristocracy as the
only social force capable of resisting the slide into commodification and conformity. Baudelaire was fascinated by the ambi-
guities, the dangers and pleasures of urban living, yet sought
to distance himself as critical observer of modernity in the
figure of the *flâneur*, who can confront commodification without being negated by it.[13] He thus sought to recognize the
power of modernity to alter the minute texture of daily life,
while himself remaining intact, and separated from the crowd.
As Benjamin says, 'it takes a heroic constitution to live modernism' (*Baudelaire*, p. 74).

When Baudelaire looked at American culture and society, he
found it typical of the materialism and mediocrity which he
associated with the hegemony of the bourgeoisie: a mob of
buyers and sellers; a headless monster. Baudelaire's analysis
of the cultural implications of American society echoed many
of the observations of Alexis de Tocqueville after his visit to
the USA in 1831.[14] The purpose of Tocqueville's visit had been
to study the workings of democracy and to assess the extent to
which it could be combined with the preservation of individual
liberty. Although Tocqueville accepted the inevitability of
democratic organization in political spheres as the only structure which could accommodate the developing social relations
of capitalism in Europe, he was very scathing about its implications in the cultural sphere. In a democracy, Tocqueville
argued, taste for the useful predominates over love of the
beautiful; novelty and superficiality replace depth and tradition; cultural production becomes subservient to the
demands of the poorly educated majority.

Thus, when Baudelaire examined the American society
against which Poe was seen as rebelling, he was invoking
twenty years of thought about the cultural limitations of capi-
talist democracy. Poe, read by Baudelaire, became an early
figure of modernism's rejection of mass culture.[15] The dichotomy thus developed – between on the one hand profundity,
linguistic complexity, and tradition, and on the other superficiality, simplification, and novelty, which was to structure so

much cultural analysis in the twentieth century – was being put in place in this very particular Franco-American intersection. Out of it emerged the figure of Poe, whose insatiable love of the beautiful, and predisposition towards the melancholy, made him the hero of Baudelaire's historical struggle against the conformity and mediocrity of mid-nineteenth-century France.

The next heroic encounter with the texts of Poe took place over one hundred years later. The author in this case was Jacques Lacan: the hero was the signifier. Lacan's seminar on 'The Purloined Letter' dates from 1956.[16] In this seminar Lacan uses Poe's tale as an illustration of his theory of the constitutive nature of the symbolic order in relation to the subject. Lacan begins by an interrogation of Freud's 'Beyond the Pleasure Principle': a text which also occurs frequently as a point of reference in *Prénoms de personne*.[17] Lacan argues that the phenomenon of 'repetition compulsion' which Freud discusses in this essay, can only be understood with reference to the symbolic order. The tendency towards obsessive repetition, which cannot be accounted for in terms of either the pleasure principle or the reality principle, must be referred to the domain of the symbolic, since this is the site where presence and absence can be maintained simultaneously. The possibility of such presence in absence within the symbolic leads to an insatiable desire for resolution of this contradiction, and thus to obsessive repetitive behaviour.[18]

Such presence in absence turns out to be the very nature of the symbolic, and in particular, of the signifier. By means of an ingenious metaphorization, Lacan reads the 'letter' of Poe's tale as a model of the working of the signifier. Lacan follows the journey of this letter: stolen from the Queen; hidden by the Minister; discovered by Dupin. He shows the complex intersubjective relations implied by the relations of different characters to this letter, and argues that the displacement of the signifier determines subjects in their actions. The purloined letter is seen as an example of the pure signifier: its message matters not at all, we do not even know what it is, but its materiality involves all subjects in the permutations of the signifying chain. Lacan argues that, in this story as in all others, the signifier only maintains itself through a displacement. Without the theft of the letter there would be no story, there would be no Dupin. The letter must leave its place in order to return, thus producing a structure of repetition which can be clearly seen in the way that Dupin duplicates in his recovery of the letter the strategies the Minister used in its theft. Lacan's readings of 'The Purloined Letter' thus amount to

> A break from naïve semanticism and naive psycho-bio-graphicism, an elaboration of a logic of the signifier (in its literal materiality and its syntactical formality), an appropriation of the problematic of *Beyond the Pleasure Principle*.[19]

Lacan adds to this reading a certain amount of speculation on the relation of the Queen to the signifier/letter, a relation characterized by shadow. He describes the place of 'woman' outside the Law, considers the similarities between the purloined letter and a female body, and observes the feminization involved in the Minister's brief possession of the letter. These speculations constitute the basis of Derrida's criticism of Lacan. In 'The Purveyor of Truth' (1975), Derrida produces a detailed criticism of Lacan's reading of Poe, based on the charge of 'phallogocentristic transcendentalism'. Basically, Derrida objects to the way in which Lacan reads 'The Purloined Letter' as an illustration of a theoretical truth discovered elsewhere, rather than as a piece of writing. He accuses Lacan of idealizing the signifier, of trying to fix it to the truth of a system or structure. Further, Derrida argues that Lacan's thoughts on the signifier in relation to sexual difference amount to the privileging of the phallus as transcendental signifier. Derrida argues for the need to move away from fixity, from the full and reassuring presence of the word, of fiction as truth. Instead, he offers a reading of 'The Murders in the Rue Morgue' which stresses the disruptive effect of a labyrinth of doubles without originals, and insists that 'the circulation of wishes and capital, of signifiers and letters' exceeds the structures of Lacan's models, and leads to the interminable supplementarity of 'dissemination' (p. 108).

Such interminable supplementarity also characterizes the debate on the significance of Poe's writing. After Derrida comes Barbara Johnson, and Marian Hobson, and Jane Gallop, each adding layers to this set of texts, inflecting the readings and challenging the arguments.[20] The heroic singularity which Baudelaire saw in Poe's texts has disappeared, to be replaced by their status as exempla of general qualities of the symbolic. This is the move that is challenged by Cixous's readings of Poe. Despite her interest in Poe's stories as expressive of particular structures of subjectivity and desire, Cixous remains intrigued by their uncanniness, and finally rejects all readings that do not leave a degree of irreducible strangeness in Poe's tales of doubles, ghosts, and perversity.

Cixous's reading, like Lacan's, begins with 'Beyond the Pleasure Principle', and she traces the terms of the struggle Freud described between forces of Life and Death in her analysis of three of Poe's tales: 'Ligeia', 'Berenice', and 'Morella'. She explores the attempt in all three of these tales to efface death, through ghosts, doubles, and obssessive repetition. In 'Ligeia' the dead wife returns in the body of her successor; in 'Morella' the dead wife is exactly reproduced in her daughter. The limit point between mortality and immortality thus inheres in the woman's body. Morella is read as 'la mort est là', and becomes the element that exceeds the (deadly) dialectic of desire and possession.[21]

Women are represented in these three tales as enigmatic, and femininity is linked to the uncanny. Poe's narrator worries about the 'mystery' of Morella's manner, and recognizes her femininity as he foresees her death: 'Yet she was a woman, and pined away daily' ('Morella', p. 184). Cixous argues, however, that these women are all marked off from the passivity and shadowiness which Lacan saw as their place, because of their relationship to knowledge. Berenice has teeth which the narrator fantasizes about as ideas; Ligeia is learned; and Morella introduces the narrator to speculative philosophy and the occult. Admittedly, these knowledges turn out to be themselves rather shadowy: we know that they exist, but we do not know what they contain. Still, in these narratives of reason risking itself to the point of dislocation, Cixous finds important explorations of the relation between the death drive and the will to know, which she sees as crucially dependent on the figure of the woman's body.

'Morella' also explores the violence, and the fetishism, of naming. The narrator refuses to name Morella's child, thus using the name of 'Morella' both as a substitution for, and a denial of, Morella's death. Yet a fetish loses its efficacity if it is not risked: desire depends on the simultaneity of the recognition and the denial of death, and thus cannot support its complete repression. Eventually, the narrator is compelled to speak the name of Morella, to give it to his child, a gesture which effaces her completely.

This reading seems to parallel much that is found in Lacan, and later in Derrida. Cixous's identification of the relation between knowledge, desire, and sexual difference is, however, significantly inflected by her attention to those texts where women are in the position of the knowledgeable, rather than of pure enigma. Cixous is not content with simply classifying the structures of Poe's writing, but goes on to see whether his writing, in its very excess and perversity, might not represent some sort of challenge to existing forms of subjectivity, desire, and sexual difference.

Cixous reads Poe's 'The Imp of the Perverse' as an anticipation of Freud's argument about the power of the unconscious death drive in 'Beyond the Pleasure Principle'. The narrator of this tale begins by speculating on the destructive psychological forces that operate on an individual, yet remain outside his control. Examples cited include the paralysis of will that leads to a self-destructive failure to act, and the motiveless desire to throw oneself over a cliff. In the narrator's own case, the imp of the perverse has worked in a very peculiar way: having safely got away with a muder, he is suddenly possessed by the desire to confess. He runs around frantically, in an attempt to exhaust the desire, but to no effect. He confesses, is arrested, and tells his story from prison, where he is about to be hanged.

The tale, for Cixous, is an excellent exploration of the workings of the unconscious, of the fragmentation of subjectivity. The power of the perverse means that the narrator must constantly risk himself, while struggling for security. Once more, the dialectic is deadly:

> Au sommet de la tension l'affirmation est l'énoncé d'une dénégation: *I am safe* se retourne en: je sais que je ne suis pas sauvé.
>
> (*Prénoms*, p. 210)

[At the height of tension, affirmation is the articulation of a denegation: 'I am safe' turns into: I know that I am not saved.]

Safety, Cixous argues, must be absolute, but the only way to confirm this is to put it at risk, and thus to continue in the destructive circuit of the perverse. Certainly this circuit is compelling. Reading Poe's story, we find ourselves placed like viewers of a Hitchcock movie: unable to condemn the murder, and frantically willing the murderer's escape.

Such articulation of the perverse is, for Cixous, potentially positive in its implications. First of all, it removes the illusion of subjective autonomy and intact identity. Secondly, however, it dramatizes the struggle between the deathly and the vital. Certainly, Cixous argues, the raven's dismal cry of 'nevermore' echoes throughout Poe's texts. Yet, in expressing the power of this cry, Poe invokes its opposite, through the mechanisms of writing: 'il faut qu'il y ait du sujet, du désir, de la vie pour que s'énonce le *nevermore*' (*Prénoms*, p. 214) [there must be subjectivity, desire, life, before the 'nevermore' can be expressed].

It is, finally, the power of Poe's writing to move beyond the rigid categories of 'love/death', or 'unconscious/conscious', which Cixous values. In 'L'autre analyste' Cixous argues, through a Deleuzian reading of Carroll and Joyce, for the importance of a form of writing that can play with the duplicity of the signifier, can invent linguistic games that will explore the mechanisms of desire as 'pure displacement of energy' (p. 217). She sees in Poe a writer who can explode, as well as explore, the destructive relations between desire and death. Poe tells us the difference between calculation and creative analysis in 'The Murders in the Rue Morgue', and his writing is on the side of the 'poeticomathematical' rather than that of prosaic categorization: he wants the overflowing of the spring, and not the contents of the well (p. 219).

CLARICE LISPECTOR

Clarice Lispector, the Brazilian novelist and short-story writer, has fascinated Cixous for over ten years. In Lispector's writing Cixous finds the embodiment of much that she has struggled to find in other literary texts, and to create in her own. In Lispector's texts Cixous finds the means to move beyond the deconstructive and towards the assertion of an alternative economy. The characteristics which Cixous focuses on include Lispector's exploration of subjectivity, her positing of alternative relations to otherness, her stylistic minimalism, and the audacity of the ethical issues with which she engages.

Cixous's first writings on Lispector appeared in 1979. These took the form of a critical essay, 'L'approche de Clarice Lispector', published in the journal *Poétique*, and a fictional text entitled *Vivre l'orange/To Live the Orange*.[22] Across these two texts Cixous developed her account of the specificity and the power of Lispector's writing. The commitment to Lispector continues in later texts such as 'Extreme Fidelity', 'Reaching the Point of Wheat', or 'A la lumière d'une pomme' [By the Light of an Apple], where Cixous explores the political implications of different attitudes towards 'the Law' and develops her theorization of the concept of libidinal economy through readings of Lispector's texts.[23]

The most striking element in Cixous's early writings about Lispector is the sense of recognition. Having established the political importance of feminine writing for women, Cixous has eventually found a woman practising such writing, with an understanding of its implications. Having theorized the limitations and dangers of dualist thought, of subjectivity based on the obliteration of the Other, Cixous suddenly discovers another woman writer exploring the same issues in fictional form. The impact of this discovery is expressed in intellectual, individual, and political terms.

Intellectually, the reading of Lispector leads Cixous to an exploration of Heidegger's concept of 'Being', and of the phenomenological demand for a return to 'the things themselves' in philosophical thought.[24] Heidegger's analysis of the phenomenological qualities of 'Being' involved a commitment to the primacy of the exploration of human Being over all other knowledges:

> The question of Being aims therefore at ascertaining the *a priori* conditions not only for the possibility of the sciences which examine entities as entities of such and such a type, and, in so doing, already operate with an under-

59

standing of Being, but also for the possibility of these ontologies themselves which are prior to the ontical sciences and which provide their foundations.[25]

Self-consciousness and metaphysical thought were, for Heidegger, simply ways of forgetting 'Being', of trying to negate time, mortality, and the necessity of choice. They also tended towards an understanding of the subject as divided from all other subjects and from the world, a world which the subject must then seek to reappropriate, categorize, and control through instrumental reason. Instead, Heidegger sought to understand subjectivity as a relational element of 'Being' which was necessarily intersubjective and always constituted by participation in the world of objects and experiences. Heidegger privileged Art as a site for the exploration of the temporal and subjective qualities of 'Being', a place where the data of experience could be explored outside preconceived epistemological constructions.

These ideas serve, for Cixous, as a bridge between her generally deconstructive commitment to an abolition of the dual hierarchized oppositions that structure political, cultural, and historical discourses and the positive project of constructing an alternative economy of representation based on 'The Art of Keeping Alive', or 'The Art of Receiving'.[26] Having theorized the political and cultural implications of the categories of thought with which we try to grasp the world, Cixous is clearly interested in the possibility of knowledges that will suspend or bypass such categorization. Having rejected what she describes as the Hegelian conception of subjectivity, with its obliteration of the Other, Cixous is also committed to the representation of alternative forms of subjectivity.

In Lispector's writing Cixous finds an attempt to represent the experience of knowledge, and the knowledge of experience, in ways that are not constrained by categorization or cultural expectation. For example, in *La Passion selon G.H.*, Lispector represents the progressive stripping away of expectation, moral assumption, and sense of self which confronts the protagonist, G.H., when she finds herself alone in a room with only a cockroach for company. In this novel we learn quite a lot about G.H.: about her profession, her class position, her past loves. Yet, Cixous argues, the strength of the novel lies in the ways in which Lispector manages to push aside such elements of character, to remove the local and the accidental. Confronted by a cockroach, an insect she has always loathed, G.H. is initially paralysed by neurotic dread. The novel reproduces in hideous, but compelling, detail the appearance and movements of the cockroach. Having believed herself alone, G.H. now has to cope with the intensity of response produced in her by another living thing. Her first response is to attempt to kill the cockroach: she fails, leaving the cockroach oozing white matter, but still living. Thus, G.H. is driven to confront quintessential otherness, a form of being that cannot be referred to her own subjectivity, or controlled by it. This, in turn, leads her to an exploration of her own fears, and of the inauthenticity of the self she has been:

> Jusqu'au moment où je vis le cafard, j'avais toujours donné un nom quelconque à ce que j'étais en train de vivre, pour pouvoir me sauver. Pour échapper au neutre j'avais depuis longtemps quitté l'être pour la personne, pour le masque humain.
>
> (*La Passion*, p. 105)

> [Until the moment when I saw the cockroach, I had always given some sort of name to what I was living through, so that I could save myself. In order to escape from neutrality, I had long since given up being in favour of personality, of the human mask.]

This rejection of the constraining masks of social identity in favour of the multiple and temporal experience of being is clearly related to Cixous's own literary and theoretical project. Lispector's dramatization of this process allows Cixous to move beyond the exploration of subjectivity undertaken in *Prénoms de personne*, with its interest in dreams, demons, and doubles. Rather than pushing, like Poe or Hoffmann, towards greater and greater excess, Lispector seems to offer a model of stylistic and ethical minimalism. This, at least, is the aspect of her writing that Cixous particularly values. Cixous praises Lispector for her scrupulous attention to the details of minuscule objects, and for her refusal to be seduced by the canons of the aesthetic into a limited concept of beauty:

61

A l'école de Clarice Lispector, nous apprenons l'approche. Nous prenons les leçons des choses. Les leçons d'appeler, de se laisser appeler. Les leçons de laisser venir, de recevoir. Les deux grandes leçons de vivre: *la lenteur et la laideur.*

(Entre l'écriture, p. 117)

[At Clarice Lispector's school, we learn how to approach. We follow courses in the general science of things. Courses in how to call, and how to let oneself be called. Courses in how to let things come, in how to receive. The two great lessons of living: *slowness and ugliness.*]

'Slowness', for Cixous, is a force which operates in opposition to the reductive properties of modernity and mass culture. It is the antithesis of dominant political and cultural discourses, which offer volume and speed of communication at the expense of knowledge and understanding. 'Ugliness' is the capacity to see the significance of that which has been excluded from representation. These values are clearly gendered for Cixous. They are the 'condition of the liberation of all of humanity kept silent, hidden, hated, beneath the peoples and their histories' (*Vivre*, p. 34). Lispector's writing thus offers a model for writing that would allow for the exploration, and the transformation, of female subjectivity:

Et il faut une attente aussi puissamment pensante, ouverte, en direction des êtres tellement proches . . . pour qu'arrive le jour où les femmes qui ont toujours été – là, viennent enfin à apparaître.

(Entre l'écriture, p. 138)

[And we will need an equally powerfully thoughtful manner of waiting, a manner that is open towards the beings who are so close . . . in order that the day may arrive when the women who have always been – there, begin at last to appear.]

The effect of this form of writing will be dramatic, akin to the disruption of Kleist's earthquake in Chile, or the guerrilla action of Cixous's 'moles':

déjà je ressentais les signes avant-coureurs d'un effondrement de grottes calcaires souterraines, s'écroulant sous le poids de couches archéologiques stratifiées – et le poids de ce premier effondrement faisait s'affaisser les coins de ma bouche et me laissait les bras ballants.

(*La Passion*, pp. 55–6)

[already I perceived the signs of an imminent collapse of underground limestone caves, falling in under the weight of stratified layers of rock – and the weight of this first collapse made the corners of my mouth give way and left my arms dangling.]

The political implications of Lispector's writing are explored in *Vivre l'orange* particularly. This text is a fictional treatment of Cixous's engagement with Lispector's texts. In it, Cixous uses the symbol of the orange: a symbol with many possible meanings, and with particular personal meanings for Cixous. The orange is at different times in the text a symbol of the qualities of Lispector's prose; an example of the kind of object which in its materiality and its seeming triviality is often left out of novelistic representations; the unconscious; the East; the Jewish people; or women.[27] It is also an image which Cixous has used very powerfully in her own fictional writing: in *Portrait du soleil* the blood-orange becomes the focus for a complex set of imagery involving blood, light, and moistness, as well as being an expression of Cixous's subjective history (a combination of 'Oran', her home town, and 'je'). Cixous insists that *'the love of the orange is political too'*, by which she means that the recognition and realization of an alternative economy of representation is potentially disruptive and liberating (*Vivre*, p. 26). It is 'the work of un-forgetting, of un-silencing, of unearthing . . . Clarice gives us the example; reminds us of the urgency, the reward' (*Vivre*, p. 78).[28]

The politics of Lispector's project also depend, for Cixous, on the representation of a different possible relation between the self and others. The Other in *La Passion selon G.H.* is, of course, a cockroach. Here the emphasis is on the capacity of G.H. to resist the desire to destroy, or to appropriate, the other living creature that necessarily impinges upon her. In *The Hour of the Star*, however, the focus is on the intersubjective relation between the narrator and the central character, Maca-

63

béa.[29] Macabéa is a poor, unattractive, unintelligent, and sickly young woman. She lives a life seemingly void of emotional significance, moving between a violent, stupid, and faithless boyfriend, an unsympathetic doctor, and a maudlin spiritualist, until she is finally run over by a yellow Mercedes and killed. Her only pleasure seems to be drinking Coca-Cola.

The appalling conditions of Macabéa's life, the hopelessness of her living conditions, the indifference of those she meets, and her final destruction by a symbol of wealth and luxury, mean that this novel could have been a document of realism, of social protest. Instead, the energy of the novel lies in the consciousness of the narrator, in his attempts to understand his relations to Macabéa. The choice of a male narrator, who draws attention to his gender: 'in the mirror there appears my own face, weary and unshaven . . . I've also had to give up sex and football', is an important distancing device, which tends to frame the whole text as an experiment in writing (*Hour*, p. 22). The narrator is aware of the apparent poverty of Macabéa as a fictional character: 'I am the only person who finds her charming. As the author, I alone love her' (p. 27), and sets about fulfilling his mandate of 'reveal[ing] her presence' (p. 19). What sustains Macabéa, and the narrative, is her instinct for survival: we become involved in the dramas of her life, and in the tragedy of her death. Throughout, however, we are reminded of the presence of the narrator, who identifies increasingly with Macabéa. Her death becomes, for him, not a tragedy but a symbol of the power of life. Macabéa dies saying 'As for the future',[30] and the narrator reflects that 'Death is an encounter with the self' (p. 85).

In 'Extreme Fidelity' Cixous argues that *The Hour of the Star* is an exploration of 'how to love the other, the strange, the unknown, the not-me-at-all' (p. 11). This non-appropriative relation to the Other is linked, by Cixous, to a transgressive relation to the Law. Retelling the story of Adam and Eve, Cixous argues that there is a different possible relation to knowledge, one that is not afraid to confront the separate existence of things, to confront their materiality, their insides: to taste the apple. This form of knowledge will not accept the abstract power of the Law. Unlike Kafka's hero, it refuses pure interdiction. It is thus related to what Cixous has theorized as the feminine economy of writing, characterized by a refusal to internalize the Law, and openness to the Other.

The imagery which Cixous uses to develop her analyses of the specificity and importance of Lispector's writing stresses themes such as 'simplicity', 'innocence', and 'poverty'. What is intended here is not, of course, naïveté. Innocence is not to be confused with ignorance, nor with moral purity. Instead, it is a sublime state , to be striven for:

> Je ne suis pas innocente. L'innocence est une science du sublime. Et je ne suis qu'au tout début de l'apprentissage. Mais je suis devant l'innocence comme une jeune fille devant l'innombrable scintillement d'une forêt dans laquelle elle brûle de plonger mais qu'elle voudrait avoir caressée feuille à feuille. Et comme le poète, devant une montagne comme devant la poésie promise, fou d'elle, désespéré d'elle mais humblement confiant en sa force de présence.
>
> (*Vivre*, pp. 26, 27)

> [I am not innocent. Innocence is a science of the sublime. And I am only at the very beginning of the apprenticeship. But in front of innocence I am like a young girl in front of the innumerable twinklings of a forest into which she longs to plunge but that she would wish to have caressed leaf by leaf. And as the poet, before a mountain as before the promised poetry, driven mad by it but humbly confident in its force of presence.]

The innocence is epistemological: it denotes a form of knowledge which is not completely enmeshed in the oppositions that structure dominant philosophical discourses, a form of knowledge explored more fully in Cixous's novel, *With ou l'art de l'innocence*. In her discussions of innocence, Cixous echoes the language of the narrator of *The Hour of the Star*, who says 'I only achieve simplicity with enormous effort' (p. 11) and says of Macabéa that 'in her poverty of body and soul one touches sanctity' (p. 21). The problem with this sort of metaphorization is that it seems to risk falling into another sort of appropriation: a figure who is stripped of all material possessions, or control over her own life, becomes a symbol of epistemological innocence and spiritual simplicity. A kind of 'orientalism' seems to operate, which reads into the fact of cultural and social difference a repository of the values repressed within western culture:[31] 'All of the orient is orange' (*Vivre*, p. 32). Anxiety about this sort of appropriation can only be increased when Cixous writes of Macabéa:

> What she has is simply living. Not the eating and drinking, which she is almost without. This poverty is her richness. It is what we do not have, we who have lost the paradise of before-lobster.
>
> ('Extreme Fidelity', p. 33)

The cultural and social position from which this seems to be articulated makes it hard to see it as a universal truth about the nature of simplicity.

The commitment that lies behind Cixous's readings of Lispector cannot, finally, be understood without some reference to the more personal and strategic dimensions of these readings. Cixous marks the importance of her encounter with Lispector very clearly:

> Une écriture est venue à pas d'ange – quand j'étais si loin de moi-même, seule à l'extrémité de mon être-finie, j'avais l'être d'écriture qui se désolait d'être si seule, qui envoyait des lettres sans adresse de plus en plus tristes.
>
> (*Vivre*, pp. 10, 11)

> [A writing came with an angel's footsteps – when I was so far from myself, alone at the extremity of my finite being, my writing-being was grieving for being so lonely, sending sadder and sadder unaddressed letters.]

Writing in 1978, Cixous talks of living in an 'over-published solitude', feeling cut off from contact with other women writers and with the imaginative energies she needs in order to write (*Vivre*, p. 48). Her theorization of 'feminine' writing had taken place almost entirely in terms of the texts of canonical male writers, such as Joyce, Kleist, or Hoffmann. Her theoretical vocabulary had been derived from Freud and Derrida. Suddenly she discovered a writer who was largely unknown in France, who was Jewish, who was a woman, and who seemed to share many of her own philosophical and stylistic preoccupations. The opportunities for a highly personal, and very committed, engagement with this writer seemed immense.

Stylistically, the relations between Cixous's and Lispector's writings are close. Both use visual imagery to powerful effect: stressing the emotional weight of colour, of texture, of sunlight, or of darkness. Both are interested in exploring the complexities of subjectivity, structuring their fictions round amorphous central characters, sometimes designated simply by initials. Lispector's exploration of the possibility of knowledge beyond categorization, her interrogation of the limits of naming – 'I ate the food and not its name' ('The Sharing of Bread', p. 30) – echoes the prolonged questioning of fixed identity in Cixous's *Le Nom d'Oedipe*. Both Lispector and Cixous rely very heavily on spatial metaphor in order to explore the limits of thought. Lispector's 'au-delà de l'oreille existe un son' [beyond the ear there exists a sound] or 'Comme si j'étais aussi, aussi côté du cube, le côté qu'on ne voit pas' [As if I were also, also a side of the cube, the side which one does not see], are reminiscent of Cixous's spatial representations of theoretical conflict in 'Sorties', or her interest in Lewis Carroll's 'other side' of the looking-glass.[32] Similarly, images of the desert, explorations of nothingness, mark both *La Passion selon G.H.* and Cixous's *Préparatifs de noces*.

The intertext of Lispector's and Cixous's texts also has a significant amount in common. Cixous points out that Lispector borrowed a phrase from Joyce's *Portrait of the Artist* as the title of her first novel, *Near to the Wild Heart*.[33] In *La Passion selon G.H.* (p. 61), we find G.H. reflecting on her identity in relation to her town, and to the world, in a way that is very like Stephen Dedalus's placing of himself in relation to school, country, and universe in *Portrait of the Artist* (p. 15). The last word of *The Hour of the Star* is 'yes', which clearly echoes the last word of Molly Bloom's monologue, in the final section of *Ulysses*. Kafka is also an important point of reference in Lispector's texts. The encounter between G.H. and the cockroach functions as a reworked version of Kafka's *Metamorphosis*, with the otherness of insect life provoking an interrogation of identity.

For Cixous, then, the encounter with Lispector's writing has proved to be a crucial part of her own writing project. Cixous found Lispector when she felt isolated as a writer and as a woman. She found in her a sustained exploration of the relations between subjectivity and writing, which echoed many of the themes and strategies she had identified in Joyce, or in Hoffmann. She also found in her a commitment to the exploration of many of the philosophical and linguistic issues that had preoccupied Cixous from the beginning of her writing career: the possibility of an alternative economy of representation related to the bodily, the overturning of hierarchies, the recognition of the multiplicity of subjectivity, and an intensity of linguistic expression which manifested itself in a stylistic minimalism. The timing of the encounter between these two women writers was impeccable, and the strategic and political implications immense:

> Je me suis laissé lire selon C.L., sa passion m'a lue, et dans le courant brûlant et humide du lire, j'ai vu comme les textes familiers et étrangers, de Rilke ou de Heidegger, ou de Derrida, avaient été lus-déjà, emportés, répondus, dans l'écrire-vivre de C.L.
>
> (*Entre l'écriture*, p. 117)

> [I let myself read in the manner of C.L., her passion read me, and in the burning and humid current of reading, I saw how the texts, both familiar and strange, of Rilke or of Heidegger, or of Derrida, had been already-read, carried along, and answered in the living-writing of C.L.]

The experience of reading Lispector's texts increased Cixous's confidence in the possibility of developing forms of writing that would not amount to pure reproduction, to the grinding inevitability of a reaffirmation of the status quo. Within her own creative writing, it allowed her to move from the interrogation of fragmentation to the assertion of the possibility of new, and sustainable, forms of subjectivity.

3

WRITING DIFFERENTLY

In her fictional writings Cixous explores many of the issues that also dominate her theoretical and critical works. Subjectivity, the corporeal roots of language, femininity, relations to the Other, and the possibilities of social and subjective transformation recur in her fictional texts as points of focus, or of tension, in texts whose radical deconstruction of linguistic and narrative structures enact the audacity of her cultural and political project. The intertextual collage of allusion, theory, and autobiographical exploration which we have found in texts such as 'La Venue à l'écriture' also forms an important element in her fictional texts, which transform, reshape, and re-invent the narratives, myths, and philosophical discourses that shape our identities.

Cixous's 'fictions' stretch the limits of the novelistic. Character is uncertain, narrative point of view unstable, the apparent transparency of language is challenged, and linear temporality is unsettled, or completely undone. Some of these techniques are already familiar from the work of other modern writers: what is specific to Cixous, however, is the intensity and extremity of her project, and its insistent questioning of the categories of sexual identity. Each of her texts pushes the limits of the representable, in a political and cultural project whose terms are constantly reworked, whose conclusions are always challenged. Thus, an affirmative text, such as *La*, which explores the constitution of a feminine subjectivity, is followed by the almost unbearable traumas and terrors of *Angst*.

Language, for Cixous, is not simply a medium for the expression of ideas and images which have their origins elsewhere. Rather, language is a material form, where signifiers, and particularly sounds, create meanings that proliferate, exceed the resources of the descriptive, offer recognitions and pleasure. Such a commitment to the density, complexity, and excess of language is more usually associated with the poetic than the novelistic, and it is indeed with 'the poetic' that Cixous allies her fictional writing:

> But only the poets – not the novelists, allies of representationalism. Because poetry involves gaining strength through the unconscious and because the unconscious, that other limitless country, is the place where the repressed manage to survive.
>
> ('Laugh of the Medusa', p. 250)

This interest in the material texture of language is related to Cixous's conviction that writing is produced, and understood, in relation to the body. By this she does not mean that there is any simple equivalence between the writing body and the written text, but rather that it is impossible to sustain the complete dichotomy between mind and body which offers the illusion of intellectual control at the cost of erasing, censoring, and hystericizing the body. This interest in the relation between language and the body leads her to an engagement with the unconscious, as the locus of that which has been repressed by the brutal severing of the corporeal and the linguistic, and by the processes of sexual differentiation. Thus both myth and dream are used in her texts as ways of exploring the archaic and the repressed, and as ways of unsettling the illusion of subjective autonomy and conscious control.

Cixous's earliest fictional text is *Le Prénom de Dieu*, a collection of short stories published in 1967. In this text she explores the sustainability of autonomous identity in the face of the violence and structural overdetermination of patriarchal social relations. The volume opens with three stories that focus on the conflicts generated within a nuclear family. Each story has a male narrator, who articulates the fears, and acts of symbolic murder, that sustain the nuclear family. 'L'outre vide' begins with the claim that 'La chair de ma mort est lisse et tendre' [The flesh of my death is smooth and soft], a claim that sets in play the paradoxical relations between the corporeal and the deadly that will inflect all of the stories in the volume (p. 9).

This story dramatizes the struggle between the narrator and the symbolic father, who tries to school him in the appropriate use of language, tries to teach him to say 'la', 'le', 'les', 'ta', when the narrator wants only to say 'moi' (p. 15). The resolution of this conflict takes place through the symbolic murder of the mother, who has shut him in within the family, locked him into a 'dedans' which threatens to consume him and destroy him. The violence in 'Le successeur' takes a more classically Oedipal form. Here the narrator has murdered the king, his father, and seeks to marry his mother. This entry into the patriarchal order brings only suffering, however, as he realizes that 'un roi est un homme mort qui parle comme un dieu' [a king is a dead man who speaks like a god] (p. 46). The inevitability of the fear and violence expressed in this story is further explored in 'La marche', which dramatizes the usurpation of the father by the son.

The stories Cixous tells in this volume are disturbing in their familiarity and their excess. The struggle to assert individuality, to achieve separation from the mother, seems to bring with it a necessary and recurring violence. The necessity for such individuation is, however, stressed in a story such as 'La ville', which is set in a future world of almost total regimentation. In this story, the 'old order' of individualism, memory, and disorder emerges as a necessary counterbalance to the trend towards homogenization and erasure of the past. 'La ville' highlights the ambiguity of the structures of subjectivity Cixous explores throughout the volume and invites speculation about the possibility of an autonomy which would not involve the obliteration of the Other. At times, the conflicts and violence she describes seem to have the inevitability of the natural, at other moments the source of the inevitability seems rather to lie in the particular social relations of patriarchy. This uncertainty reflects a tension endemic to psychoanalysis, and is accentuated by Cixous's use of Biblical and mythical texts, which seem to carry the weight of a truth outside history.

The possibility of challenging the social and subjective relations of patriarchy is implicit in some of the stories in the volume. 'Le veau de plâtre' is a reworking of Kafka's *Metamorphosis*, where the narrator finds himself encased in plaster. This metamorphosis creates a crisis in his relation to the bodily, allows him to see beneath the surface of identities, and provokes a radical questioning of the values of his life. He struggles to achieve a coherent perspective on the people who surround him, 'Je voulais voir le dos des êtres' [I wanted to see the back of other beings], but this leads him to a complete rejection of the 'life' that has been his (p. 120). Concluding that his death would be more lively than the life he has been enduring, he says, 'Je me laissai aller à mon absence sans angoisse' [I let myself drift into my own absence without anguish], a scandalous statement, where the use of the past historic tense serves to invite a reading of the death as symbolic (p. 137).

The only story which really challenges the inevitability of patriarchal violence, however, is 'Le lac'. This story focuses on the plight of a young girl after the death of her parents. Rejecting the fixed identities of 'daughter' and 'sister', she undertakes a journey in search of an identity outside 'l'ombre des autres' [the shadow of others] (p. 143). She travels inside herself, finding not confinement and enclosure but a self which is more extensive than she could have guessed. Arriving by the shore of a lake, she falls asleep, and, in a dreamlike revelation discovers that 'elle était la lune, la lumière et la nuit, l'ultime et l'initiale, la question et la réponse' [she was the moon, the light and the darkness, the end and the beginning, the question and the answer] (p. 152). Laughing, she reads a letter from the father, from God, which tells her to create her own identity, to live her own life, to suppress his power.

The subjective and interior journey of the daughter through language also forms the basis of Cixous's novel *Dedans*, which was published in 1969.[1] This autobiographical novel explores a young girl's reaction to her father's death, and to the family relations in which she is initially both placed and defined. In a compelling narrative of the compulsions and pleasures of Oedipal relations, as well as of their destructiveness, Cixous writes of a journey through patriarchy and language, and towards a rejection of the dead weight of a subjective economy of mutual destruction.

Spatial metaphor is a crucial element of the structure of this novel. The 'inside' of the title takes many forms. Firstly, it refers to the family home, in which she finds herself enclosed:

MA MAISON EST ENCERCLEE. ELLE EST ENTOUREE PAR LE

GRILLAGE. DEDANS, nous vivons. Dehors ils sont cinquante mille, ils nous encerclent. Dedans je suis quand même chez nous: je suis sûre qu'ils n'oseront pas rentrer.

(p. 11)

[MY HOUSE IS SURROUNDED. IT IS ENCIRCLED BY THE IRON GRATING. INSIDE, we live. Outside, they are fifty thousand, they surround us. Inside, all the same, I'm home: I'm sure they will not dare come in.

(p. 7)]

The image is one of imprisonment, but also one of security, and this is the conflict that dominates the novel. 'Inside' represents an enclosure: in the past, the house had been open, but her father had enclosed it. This is the 'inside' from which the narrator needs to escape, a space which is entirely defined by the father, which presents itself as self-sufficient, lacking nothing but 'laitages' ['dairy products'] (p. 14/p. 9). As the novel progresses, this enclosed space becomes a prison, into which she is invited by her male lovers, who promise her pleasure, security, and passion, if she will only say 'Je suis tout ce que tu voudras' ['I'm anything you want me to be'] (p. 174/p. 113).

This sense of imprisonment is perpetually undermined, or at least complicated, by the other associations of 'inside' developed within the novel. Thus 'inside' also comes to represent the Imaginary, and that space which is before language, where identity is fluid and the self is ubiquitous. Unusually, this space is associated with the father, whose bodily presence sustains the imagination of the young girl, as well as with the warmth and darkness of her mother's bed. Against this 'inside' is the world of language, knowledge, names, and time, which we could relate to the properties of the Symbolic. These dimensions of the Imaginary and the Symbolic are further developed as figures of 'identification' and 'separation' throughout the novel, as the narrator tries to construct a form of subjectivity that acknowledges difference while sustaining a relation with the Other.

The 'inside' of this text can also be understood as a matter of historical and cultural identity. The narrator is inside the Jewish identity of her family: a position that offers her powerful recognitions and pleasures, but also allies her with her grandmother, whose marriage offered her only enclosure and the occasional relief of wishful thinking. The 'insideness' is also necessarily partial: much of the novel is set in North Africa, where her Jewishness and her Frenchness constitute problematic identities of marginality and power. The anxieties surrounding cultural identity are signalled in the second part of the novel where the now-adult narrator is bombarded by questions:

> Un autre interroge: 'Quand êtes-vous née? Où êtes-vous née? Quel est le motif de votre visite? Combien de temps? Où? Avec qui? Pourquoi? . . .'
>
> (p. 149)

> [Another one interrogates me: 'When were you born? Where were you born? What is the reason for your visit? For how long? Where? With whom? Why? . . .'
>
> (p. 97)]

The final associations with the 'inside' are with the corporeal dimensions of the self. The body offers no security of identity in this novel, with its images of bodily fragmentation and carnal destruction:

> Ensuite j'aurais bougé; j'aurais ouvert la veine dans la tempe, et j'aurais bu, sucé, aspiré, et j'aurais léché ses paupières et le blanc de ses yeux et j'aurais mis mes doigts partout . . .
>
> (p. 184)

> [Afterwards I would have done something; I would have opened the vein in his temples, and I would have drunk, sucked, inhaled, and I would have licked his eyelids and the whites of his eyes and I would have put my fingers all over . . .
>
> (p. 120)]

The anatomy textbook she studies with her mother, with its clearly segmented and categorized body, a 'man' who is supposed to represent the human body, is rejected as misleading. Yet the body does also seem to offer a kind of truth, a force that cannot be completely contained and constantly threatens to exceed its limits. The flesh remembers, and resists: 'la chair est moins bête que l'esprit, elle n'oublie pas' ['the body is not as big a fool as the mind, it doesn't forget'] (p. 88/p. 57), and the internal depths of the corporeal offer resources that will challenge the alienation and fragmentation brought about by the father's language:

> J'ai peu de mots. Mon père qui les avait tous, est parti si précipitamment, qu'il n'a pas eu le temps de me les donner . . . Ils divisaient ce qui m'avait toujours paru fait d'une seule pièce. Mes doigts étaient hachés en phalanges, ma main, que je trouvais belle et vive, était découpée, articulée, lointaine.
>
> (p. 52)

> [I don't have many words. My father, who had them all, left in such a hurry that he didn't have time to give them to me . . . They divided up what had always seemed to be whole. My fingers were chopped up into joints, my hand, which to me was beautiful and alive, was carved up, jointed, far away.
>
> (pp. 32–3)]

At first, the relations between 'inside' and 'outside' are conceived of as a struggle, a fight to the death. Yet, as the novel progresses, we are moved towards a different understanding of these spatial relations. To be completely 'outside' is impossible and dangerous, yet to accept the limitations of the 'inside' is equally untenable. Instead, in a move that echoes Nietzsche's *Beyond Good and Evil*, and Freud's *Beyond the Pleasure Principle*, Cixous tries to move us to a space 'beyond' the dichotomy between inside and outside. Her aim is neither to be trapped in the Imaginary, nor silenced by the Symbolic.

At an early age, the narrator refuses the arbitrary imposition of power:

> J'affirme être un chien libre, mon frère affirme qu'il n'y a pas de chien sans corde, et pas de corde sans maître. Mais, dit mon frère en baissant la tête, on ne voit pas le maître parce qu'il est toujours derrière.
> – Alors, comment sais-tu qu'il est là?
> – La corde.
>
> (p. 39)

[I insist on being a free dog, my brother insists there is
no such thing as a dog without a leash, and no leash
without a master. But, says my brother, lowering his
head, you can't see the master because he is always
behind you.
—Then how do you know he's there?
—The leash.

(p. 24)]

She refuses to internalize the Law, and tries to fly free of the
fetters that hold her to the 'inside'. Her journey beyond the
confines of her gender and her history is traumatic. By the
second part of the novel she can begin by saying 'Je suis' ['I
am'], but this sense of self is constantly eroded by the erotic
relations that fill her early adult years.

She realizes that any movement beyond the oppositions of
'inside' and 'outside' will involve her in an interrogation of
difference and of sexuality. She details the subjective dissol-
ution suffered by the women in her family: her father's mother
is reduced to a passive mirror of his developing identity. Yet
her own position in these Oedipal dramas is unclear: like
Electra, she is at times the 'arch phallocrat', hating her mother
and struggling to bring back the dead father. At other times
she rejects the categories of sexual difference completely:

La seule différence incontestable n'est pas celle des sexes
ou des âges ou des forces, mais celle des vifs et des
morts.

(p. 121)

[The only incontestable difference is not that of sex or
age or strength, but that of the living and the dead.

(p. 79)]

But even this opposition does not stand up, as the young
narrator uses language to erase her father's death, by insisting
on thinking about him in the present tense.

In the end, the narrator is nearly destroyed by the weight
of these contradictions, by the desire to inhabit a space that
has no reality beyond the allusive quality of the 'beyond'. She
tries to move beyond the categories and limitations of language, but can do so only linguistically. She tries to escape

from the enclosure of the 'inside' only to return to its apparent
security. She tries to refuse the oppositions of sexual identity,
but is confronted by the disruption caused by the multiplicity
and excess of her own subjectivity which will acknowledge
neither the master nor the leash. When in a moment of sexual
pleasure, she risks a journey beyond her own apparent limits,
her lover is terrified:

> Voilà ce qu'elle faisait, comme si lui n'avait pas existé.
> Elle pouvait faire n'importe quoi. Il fallait s'attendre à
> n'importe quoi; il en avait les yeux qui bondissaient en
> tous sens. A la fin il ne se souvenait plus de la différence
> entre la droite, le bas, le haut, la gauche, le sud,
> l'ouest . . . je rassemblai toutes mes poules dans un quad-
> rillage serré, et j'eus la joie de sentir que j'étais toujours
> un homme; rien ne me faisait peur; ma force musculaire
> fidèle, ma verge aussi. J'étais toujours là.
>
> (pp. 202–3)

> [This is what she did, as if he had never existed. She
> was capable of anything. You could expect anything from
> her; it made his eyes dart about every which way. In the
> end he no longer remembered the difference between
> right, bottom, top, left, south, west . . . I gathered all my
> hens in a tight little grid, and I knew the joy of feeling
> I was still a man; nothing could make me afraid; my
> muscular strength stood by me, my penis too. I was still
> there.
>
> (pp. 131–2)]

The confusion of narrative voice here accentuates the sense of
crisis, which culminates in the young woman's final return to
her home.

At home, she tries on an old dress, and prepares, once
more, to meet her father. In a dreamlike state, she encounters
another version of herself, a self that wants to hold her back,
to stop her going through the door. When she finds her father,
she fantasizes about their identity as the 'eternal couple', yet
quickly rejects such erasure of herself:

> Or j'en ai marre des bords de mort et j'en ai marre des
> remplaçants. Et bien que je sois la princesse des avant-

77

temps, et la fille d'un dieu mort, et la maîtresse des inscriptions tombales, des livres de pierre, des robes de mer, je ne suis pas contente . . . je me réjouis de pouvoir parler, que j'aie dix ans, trente ans ou soixante, et de pouvoir dire merde merde merde à la mort.

(p. 208)

[Now I'm sick and tired of standing at the shores of death and I'm sick and tired of substitutes. And though I am the princess of anterior time and the daughter of a dead god, and the mistress of tombstone inscriptions, of books of stone, of seawater gowns, I am not happy . . . I rejoice in my power to speak, in the fact that I am ten years old, thirty years old or sixty, and that I can say kiss off kiss off to death.

(p. 135)]

She thus rejects the limitations of her space within the deadly economy of the absent father at the same time that she craves it. That final rejection of death carries the weight of her speaking self, and echoes of both the mother ['la mère'] and the sea ['la mer'].

Although this seems like the emotional climax of the novel, it is not, in fact, its conclusion. A brief paragraph follows this rejection of death, where the narrator once more places herself 'inside'. She enters prison, and finds a kind of peace, though one that cannot dispel the disruption of the novel as a whole. In a space beyond words, beyond sexual difference, and beyond time, and through total identification with the Other, we are offered the possibility of a 'dedans' where 'nous aurons cessé de mourir' ['we shall have stopped dying'] (p. 209/p. 136).

Cixous's exploration of the 'beyond' extended across a number of texts published in the early 1970s. *Le Troisième Corps*, *Les Commencements*, *Neutre*, *Tombe*, and *Portrait du soleil* all use techniques of intertextual collage to disturb the expectations of novelistic structure and to challenge the adequacy of rational thought and conscious identity. Each of these texts involves a journey of exploration by a subject, a 'je', whose contradictory and painful confrontation with theoretical discourse and with literary and artistic representations constitutes the drama of the text. As Nicole Ward Jouve has argued, each of these texts displays 'the inner logic of a psychoanalytic cure'.[2] Freud, Kleist, and Poe provide some of the points of reference, with their texts of the uncanny, the dreamlike, and the perverse. Yet no single writer provides the 'key' to any one of these texts, whose subjective complexity, temporal transgression, and dialogic structure render any summary impossible.

Such is the strangeness of these texts that the question of how to read them becomes pressing. They have many stories, but no overall narrative. No single character offers a way through the text as a whole: characters transform themselves throughout the texts, and have, at best, a symbolic focus. They also seem to avoid the impulse towards an ambitious mythological resolution, which renders many modernist texts ultimately readable. Gilles Deleuze, considering the theoretical and literary problems raised by these early texts of Cixous, has suggested the development of a new practice of reading, which he calls 'stroboscopic'.[3] By this, he means that her work should be read once quickly, and then re-read. The 'difficulties' of a slow reading, Deleuze argues, disappear in this first encounter with the text, where associations between different elements combine in a surprising way that echoes the effect of rapid but discontinuous lighting.

Much of the effect of this complexity, rapidity, and disruption is, of course, diminished by the application of critical discourse to these texts, whose multiplicity functions as a deliberate challenge to the critic who strives after coherence, organicism, and conclusion. None the less, it does seem important to attempt a reading that will move beyond the simple registering of a general response to such disruptive texts. In clarifying the cultural and theoretical intertext of one of these novels, *Portrait du soleil* [Portrait of the Sun], then, my aim is to suggest ways of reading Cixous's fiction that relate it to the rest of her work, without reducing it to the illustration or dramatization of an already-arrived-at position.

This novel opens with the statement 'Il faut choisir une sanguine' [It is necessary to choose a blood-orange], and proceeds to set in play a range of associations between blood, light, language, and subjectivity which set the tone of the novel.[4] The orange, so important to Cixous's discussion of Lispector, is here written 'oranje': a combination of Cixous's place of birth, Oran, and the first-person pronoun, 'je'. 'Oranje', the narrator says, is the first word she ever dissected, in order to uncover its hidden meanings and subjective ramifications. Word-play is, indeed, an important element in the novel, where 'jeudi' [Thursday] becomes 'jeudit' [gamesaid], and February becomes 'fièvrier', with its implications of feverishness (p. 5).

The orange is the first image that suggests the complex of meanings associated with the sun in this novel. The 'sanguine', in linking blood and orange, leads to a consideration of the bodily dimensions of subjectivity, to the claim by the narrator that her blood speaks. These images of light, blood, and corporeal identity are then linked to one of the symbolic characters in the novel: Dieubis, a kind of second God, who tempts, and terrifies, the narrator.

Dieubis is contrasted with, but sometimes mingles with, the character of Jeor. Jeor's name suggests a form of subjectivity, as well as the name of Cixous's own father, Georges. Jeor is the character who seems to hold out the promise of a stable identity for the narrator, who longs to erase the power of Dieubis's associations with the ancient and the bloody. It is tempting to read these two characters as a continuation of the Oedipal scenario that was so important to *Le Prénom de Dieu* and *Dedans*. To some extent this is licensed by the observation that 'Dieubis a quelque chose de vague en commun avec la mer' [Dieubis has something vaguely/wave-like in common with the sea/the mother] (p. 9), and by the promises and threats that Jeor seems to represent for the narrator. The security of this symbolic couple is however disrupted by the introduction of a number of other characters, including Freud, Dora, and the mythical Dioniris.

'Dioniris', who also appeared in Cixous's novel *Tombe*, is a compound of the Egyptian god Osiris, who was murdered, brought back to life, and then ruled in the underworld, and Dionysus, the Greek god of excess and misrule. The invocation of Dionysus here opens the text out towards a series of philosophical and literary discussions of the Dionysian, as a force of transgression and a repository of cultural energy. Cixous explores such concepts of the violent and the excessive throughout her early fictional writing, drawing heavily on the texts of Nietzsche and of Georges Bataille.

In his exploration of the origins of tragedy, Nietzsche had described the different forces that competed within the world of Greek tragedy by reference to the gods Dionysus and Apollo. These gods were used to represent the conflict between forces of excess and violence and those of order and reason. The Dionysian aspect of Greek culture, Nietzsche argued, had been dangerously underplayed, in the interests of a version of human culture which stressed the individual, the spiritual, and the rational over the violent and the irrational.

The extent to which Nietzsche's writings provided a theoretical and stylistic source for Cixous's early work is clear when we examine a passage such as 'Of the Despisers of the Body', where Nietzsche writes:

> You say 'I' and you are proud of this word. But greater than this – although you will not believe in it – is your body and its great intelligence, which does not say 'I' but performs 'I'.[5] *Thus spoke Zarathustra p.62*
> *cf. Bray p. 56*

However, it is his discussion of the Dionysian that provides the most useful point of entry to *Portrait du soleil*. The unsettling, compelling, and exhausting experience of reading this novel is caught very precisely in Nietzsche's description of an encounter with the Dionysian:

> For the rapture of the Dionysian state with its annihilation of the ordinary bounds and limits of existence contains, while it lasts, a *lethargic* element in which all personal experiences of the past become immersed. This chasm of oblivion separates the worlds of everyday reality and of Dionysian reality. But as soon as this everyday reality re-enters consciousness, it is experienced as such, with nausea: an ascetic, will-negating mood is the fruit of these states.[6]

Cixous derives from Nietzsche, then, a commitment to moving beyond the categories of the rational and the knowable, towards the site of creation, multiple subjectivity, and the bodily roots of human culture. Such a commitment is also clear in the work of Bataille, whose writings are frequently alluded to in *Portrait du soleil*. In the Preface to *La Part maudite* [The Accursed Share], published in 1967, Bataille had posed the question, 'how can we solve the enigma, how can we measure up to the universe, if we content ourselves with the slumber of conventional knowledge?', a question which echoes the radical reformulations implicit in Cixous's writing.[7] Bataille's text contains a consideration of Mauss's work on 'the gift', which was clearly important for the development of Cixous's own thinking about this concept. His discussion of 'the gift' leads him on to a more general formulation of the concept of 'dépense' [spending and unthinking], and allows him to consider those aspects of human culture that are not reducible to the classical economic balance between production and consumption: aspects including war, games, spectacles, art, and perverse sexuality. Such activities, Bataille argues, show the futility of a mechanical systematization of human existence. One of Bataille's privileged examples of 'dépense' is the action of the sun:

> The origin and essence of our wealth are given in the radiation of the sun, which dispenses energy – wealth – without any return. The sun gives without ever receiving.
> (*The Accursed Share*, p. 28)

The sun, both for Cixous and for Bataille, is on the side of energy, of giving without a thought for return, of the uncontainable. The desire to construct a 'portrait' with its implications of framing and fixed perspective, seems, thus, bound to fail. Cixous acknowledges the problem in her allusion to Rembrandt's painting of *The Anatomy Lesson of Dr Tulp*. This painting represents an anatomical demonstration, with a corpse surrounded by willing scholars. The arm of the corpse has already been dissected, showing flesh and blood vessels of a hideous colour, which contrast with the luminous whiteness of the corpse, and the staid clothes of the scholars and the doctor. The narrator of *Portrait du soleil* rejects Rembrandt's representation of the body, saying its geometrical precision renders the corpse doubly dead, by enclosing it, making of it a fixed and passive spectacle. Such practice is contrasted with the aspirations of the narrator, who seeks to understand the body as living, as multiple, as impossible to pin down: any portrait she draws will be transient, and unfinished.

Such transience is linked to the complex spatial dimensions of the novel. Part of the action takes place in Rembrandt's

Amsterdam, which has been transformed into Masterdam, other parts are set in Freud's Vienna, and yet others in a mythical Egypt. Each of these spaces carries a weight of symbolic meanings for the narrator, and each is a necessary part of her journey through the contradictions of the symbolic. The sun is most frequently associated with Egypt, with the south, with lightness, but, like the sands of Egypt, such associations shift uneasily throughout the text. Vienna is the site of the unconscious and the hysterical, of Freud and Dora.

Cixous's interest in Freud's Case History is to last through a number of fictional, dramatic, and theoretical texts. In this text, Dora functions to some extent as an exteriorization of the narrator, with Dora's hysterical cough seeming like the only possible response to the discovery that 'à l'intersection des contradictions j'étouffai, elles m'étranglaient' [at the point of intersection of the contradictions I suffocated, they were strangling me] (p. 16). At other times, Dora is the figure who has the courage to resist, to undermine Freud's discourse, and thus provides some sort of protection against the dogmatic political voices which tell the narrator 'que j'ai manqué le train de la révolution, que j'ai l'inconscient plus gros que l'estomac' [that I've missed the boat for the revolution, that my unconscious is bigger than my belly] (p. 105). Throughout the novel we hear the cough, which comes not just from Dora but also from Jeor, and signals a point of resistance. The narrator's dilemma is how this form of resistance can be integrated into the modern world, how Dora's courage can survive the pack of lions that prowl through the pass from Dora's world to her own.

The encounter with Dora leads the narrator towards a consideration of the ways in which gender shapes the dimensions of her struggle to achieve a place within the symbolic which is not a place of murder and silence: the image of throat-cutting recurs in the text, as a reminder of one way of curing Dora's cough. The consideration of this problem is not really developed within the text, and takes the form rather of an expression of the narrator's fascination with, but distance from, the expected sites of women's identity. Thus she returns to her native North Africa, and watches women kneading bread – a pleasurable activity from which she is excluded. What she is left with is a legacy of shame, and a commitment to exceed

83

the structures in which her desire and her identity would be placed by the voices and texts which bombard her. The narrator knows the stakes are high: Cixous has spoken elsewhere of the fact that women are more open to risk, since they have less to lose, but in this text we are confronted with the very real danger of eradication. 'Il y a peur et moi' [there is fear and me], says the narrator, and this fear circulates and increases throughout the novel (p. 8).

As the narratives and dreams multiply throughout *Portrait du soleil*, we encounter a version of what Freud described as 'the uncanny'. Both familiarity and strangeness are associated with these dreams of missed trains, of exams not taken, of meetings which never take place. The narrator struggles to construct a new place in which she can negotiate the contradictions that surround her and subsume her. She looks for the crack in the text, for that space that will allow her to develop a new sort of relation to the power of the phallus, and to the patriarchal culture by whose texts she is constantly interpellated. The end of the novel seems hopeful as the narrator enters the house of the Prosecutor, willing to push further, to defy fate, and finds that the Prosecutor is absent, but his wife is there to offer her compassion and gentleness. Yet the Prosecutor also turns up, and the result is violence:

Le Procureur. D'un geste, Sa main en ellipse. Se rapproche. Ralentit. Se Procureur. Coupe. D'un coup. Sec. La Gorge. Du Sujet . . . Ma gorge. Et maintenant des yeux, des yeux, des yeux, pour pleurer, pour voir où pleurer pour voir qui pleure! *Et maintenant, de quel sang signer ça?*
(p. 195)

[The Prosecutor. In one movement. His hand curved like an ellipse. Approaches. Slows down. Prosecutor of self. Cuts. With one slash. Hard. The Throat. Of the Subject . . . My throat. And now some eyes, some eyes, some eyes, to weep, to see where to weep, to see who is weeping! *And now, in what blood should that be signed?*]

The novel concludes with violence, suffering, and disabling subjective uncertainty; the movement to the 'beyond' has been only partially, and tentatively, successful.

The exploration of new spaces, beyond the confinement of

a patriarchal 'inside', is pushed much further in Cixous's novel *La*, which was first published in 1976. Here intertextual reference, multiple subjectivity, and syntactical innovation are combined with a thoughtful and humorous reworking of mythic narratives and spaces, to produce a text of playfulness and audacity.

The major intertextual reference in *La* is to the Egyptian *Book of the Dead*.[8] This book is a collection of magical texts and illustrations, a selection of which the Egyptians placed with their dead, in order to facilitate their journey through the underworld and towards eternal life. The *Book of the Dead* contains a wide range of such magical texts, dating from different historical periods, and addressing different dangers facing the dead in their journey through the underworld. The underworld, which was ruled over by Osiris, was seen as an enclosed space, whose doors the dead person had to succeed in opening. Spells were designed for the dead person to obtain a mouth, to have his mouth opened so that he could breathe once more, to avoid having his heart stolen, and to counteract putrefaction of the body.

These rituals of preparation for a space beyond the deadly are exploited by Cixous in the first section of *La*, which is called 'Le livre des mortes' [The Book of the Dead Women]. She uses the range of physical and emotional preparations suggested in the *Book of the Dead* as an indication of the difficulty and the extremity of her own desire to reach, through writing, a space of self-recognition and openness to the Other.

Cixous's use of Egyptian mythology represents an important strategic reworking of the mythic sources of western culture. By re-introducing the imagery and rituals of Egyptian religion, she is challenging the adequacy of Greek legend as a cultural origin. The importance of such undoing of cultural origins has been very convincingly argued by Martin Bernal in *Black Athena*.[9] Bernal demonstrates the political interests that lay behind the suppression of the Egyptian influence on Greek civilization, and offers his own account of the importance of Egyptian cultural forms and practices for the Greeks not just as an intellectual reappraisal, but as a means 'to lessen European cultural arrogance' (p. 73). That such disturbing of mythic origins can have particular meanings in relation to a feminist writing practice can be seen in the work of the poet H.D., whose decision to explore the narrative of 'Helen in Egypt' amounted to an indictment of the Greeks for staging their epic battle over an illusion – a Helen who was not even in Troy.[10]

In *La*, the woman who finds herself in the region of the dead is, at first, divided and overwhelmed by her precarious identity. She wonders who will burst forth from her mouth when her words come to be weighed. She tries to come to terms with the dreams that surround her without seeming to include her. She expresses a nostalgia for her previous identity: 'O mes anciens corps, mes souffles, mes jours d'avant' [O my former bodies, my earlier breaths and days] (p. 7). Her earlier knowledges seem to be of no use: the Cartesian *'cogito'* cannot withstand the pressure of such subjective splitting. Instead, she seeks the terms for new knowledges, for the spells that will carry her safely through the underworld, where women have been placed by the dominant culture, towards a different form of subjectivity and identity based on bisexuality and the consequent re-entry of femininity into the cultural and political sphere.

For this journey the woman knows that she will need new theoretical and political baggage, since 'Les vieux mots ne marchent plus' [The old words don't work any more] (p. 23). Representations of women from philosophical texts haunt this chapter, particularly Kierkegaard's assessment that before encountering love, women are nothing other than dreams. The narrator plays with this idea, undoing the marginalization it suggests by insisting on the strength and the disruption of unconscious thought. Her enquiries are facilitated by the presence of another, unknown, woman who leads her to the power inherent in a relation of identification, a limitlessness that precedes separation:

> On ne s'éveille qu'au contact de l'amour. Et avant ce temps, on n'est que jardins sans douleurs, espaces fourm-illant de corps érotiques, champs de mers poissonneuses, chairs sans soucis . . .
>
> (p. 59)

[One wakes only to the touch of love. Before then, we are only gardens without sorrows, spaces swarming with erotic bodies, landscapes of seas full of fish, flesh without cares . . .]

The intensity of such imaginary identifications leads the narrator to a consideration of the nature of sexual difference. What is it, she asks, that she recognizes in this woman she has never seen before, and what is it that woman sees in seeing herself? The answer to these questions will lead her beyond the intensity of individual identification, through separation and loss, and towards the mediation of other women.

The dimensions of this exploration of sexual difference, corporeality, and subjectivity are already suggested in the multiple ramifications of the title of this novel, *La*.[11] The title, at an obvious level, suggests both the feminine definite article and the feminine pronoun, 'la', as well as the French word for 'there': 'là'. Christiane Makward suggests that the ramifications of 'là' are both spatial and conceptual, denoting a space that is far away, yet visible, conceivable. Makward also draws attention to the musical expression 'donner le la' ['to give an A'], whose allusion to musicality and gift, and suggestion of the English 'A', the letter that both begins and ends this novel, ties in with the stylistic and thematic concerns of the novel. She also argues that *La* might be read as an answer to Lacan's emphatic statement that 'Il n'y a pas *La* femme': a negation which places woman outside the symbolic.[12] To this, we might add a possible allusion to the textual innovations of Joyce's *A Portrait of the Artist as a Young Man*, where we find the young artist and transgressor of the law dancing to a tune rendered as:

> Tralala lala,
> Tralala tralaladdy
> Tralala lala
> Tralala lala.
>
> (p. 7)

Finally, Verena Conley argues for a close connection between the text of *La*, and Derrida's *Glas*: a text which explores the representation of relations between the family, the State, and death in the writing of Hegel and of Sophocles.[13] Although this association is suggestive, and certainly licensed both by coincidence of signifier and of theme, this turn to Derrida does

tend to erase the political and theoretical importance of Cixous's movement from Greek to Egyptian culture as the site of
her fictional exploration.

As the text of *La* develops, we become increasingly aware
of the emotional and intellectual power of its idiosyncratic
symbolism. In a manner reminiscent of imagist poetry, Cixous
creates a density of meanings around a small number of
images, whose reworking facilitates the kind of theoretical and
emotional transformations she is trying to achieve in the novel.
Thus fish swim throughout the novel, suggesting unfettered
movement and an exploration of the depths, as well as the
danger of being caught, lured by the bait. The island of Mad-
eira becomes a symbol of the material, of the soil, of the
mother: associations derived from puns (*Materia, Mater, Ma
terre*), but developed into the texture of the novel as a whole.

Such density of symbolism is accompanied by a thoroughly
transgressive, and often humorous, attitude towards syntactical and stylistic consistency. Christiane Makward has identified
eleven different styles of writing in the novel, ranging from
the messianic and the liturgical to the lyric–erotic and the
surrealist. This proliferation of writing styles constantly dis-
rupts the experience of reading the novel, provokes a consideration of the role of irony and parody, and destabilizes the
narrative voice. Cixous's attitude towards grammatical structure is equally unsettling:

> Me vois sortir – le dos droit, la démarche rapide, l'amour
> l'a réveillée, l'appelle à elle, au jour demain – à main
> gauche au fond du salon – au même moment me vois
> entrer.

> (p. 39)

> [See myself go out – back straight, striding quickly, love
> has awakened her, calls her to her(self), into the light
> tomorrow – on the left-hand side at the far end of the
> lounge – at the same moment see myself enter.]

The grammatical uncertainties in this passage express some of
the conceptual complexities of the novel. It is not really possible to decide whether the seeing is being done by the narrator,
or by an unknown other; nor is it clear whether the narrator
is being called to herself or to another woman: in the end, of

course, the novel will suggest that it comes to the same thing. Cixous alludes to Nietzsche's remark that 'I fear we are not getting rid of God because we still believe in grammar'[14] and goes on to suggest that such belief, and such fear, must be challenged by a writing that will undermine the apparent relations between grammatical structure and the real world (p. 269).

But we must now return to the new arrival in the land of the dead, whom we last saw transfixed by the resources of intense identification. Despite the excess of signification, and absence of narrative structure, in this novel, there is a powerful sense of the dramatic. We want to see the new arrival escape from the confines of the underworld. The brief appearance of Dora, figured in the 'daurade' [sea bream] does not bode well. The protagonist does, however, have access to the four powers of femininity, which include the power to be both yesterday and today, and the power to come and go in her own unconscious (p. 89).

At times, the text offers a glimpse into the implications of such powers, in its images of flight, of music, of food, of the body, and of sexual desire. The emphasis here is on the limitless, the strong-willed: the convolvulus that clings, and grows, and aspires to climb ever higher. Yet there is also separation and loss, and the risk of betrayal: the Song of Songs becomes the Blood of Bloods (p. 179), and the Biblical text:

> Behold, you are beautiful, my love,
> behold you are beautiful!
> Your eyes are doves behind your veil.
> Your hair is like a flock of goats moving down the
>   slopes of Gilead.
>
> Your teeth are like a flock of shorn ewes
> that have come up from washing,
> all of which bear twins,
> and not one among them is bereaved
> (Song of Songs 4; i-ii)

is answered in Cixous's text by the plaintive 'où sont tes chèvres? Qu'as-tu fait de tes agnelles pleines de jumeaux?' [where are your goats? What have you done with your ewes which bear twins?] (p. 180).

Even in this audacious text, the burden of sustaining an identity which admits others without seeking to eradicate them, and acknowledges the sexual plurality implicit in the image of 'une belle jeune mère masculine' [a beautiful young masculine mother] is a heavy one (p. 87). There is always a watchman, a policeman, ready to intervene, and to punish.

In the last section, Cixous struggles to represent the power that comes from collective identity, and collective transgression:

> Culturally speaking, women have wept a great deal, but once the tears are shed, there will be endless laughter instead. Laughter that breaks out, overflows, a humour no one would expect to find in women – which is nonetheless surely their greatest strength because it's a humour that sees man much further away than he has ever been seen. Laughter that shakes the last chapter of my text La, 'she who laughs last'. And her first laugh is at herself.[15]

Yet images of the Fall compete with the aspiration to flight throughout this chapter. The narrator imagines the story of Adam and Eve rewritten by the snake, but then remembers that the snake had no access to writing. Explorations of the libidinal resources of bisexuality are challenged by the normative discourse of psychoanalysis.

Despite these set-backs, however, the narrator gains confidence. She feels able to dispense with the ancient goddesses she relied on to begin her journey out of the underworld of the repressed. In fact, she seems to require no resources apart from the other women who have made the journey before her, and the power of her own body: she needs no trapeze to help her fly since 'je suis moi-même le trapèze et le trapéziste' [I myself am both the trapeze and the trapezist] (p. 256).

Whether such optimism is justified is unclear. The narrator's first attempts to climb, to fly, to escape from the enclosed chamber of the dead, meet with no success, cramped as she is by the domestic architecture of the modern city. Instead, she pins her hopes on the 'Tour Effelle', a feminized monument which will be her launching pad. She does not doubt the efficacy of the theoretical and subjective skills she has acquired in the novel, yet her final triumphant flight can only be imagined in an as-yet-unrealized future:

> Sans ailes s'éloigner du perchoir, sans l'angoisse, avec elles, passer avec ses âmes, ses formes et toutes ses lettres à l'infinie où elle prendra son là.

(p. 278)

> [To move away from the perch without wings, without the anguish, with the women, to go with her souls, her forms and all her letters into the feminine infinite where she will take her *là*.]

The optimism of this intended flight is immediately problematized in Cixous's next novel, *Angst*.[16] This novel explores the pain and anguish of separation and loss with a rawness that renders it at times almost unreadable. The narrator explores the paralysing violence and fear produced by her relation to dominant forms of subjectivity, with an intensity that forces her to challenge and reject the identities available to her: 'Si tu ne meurs pas le cœur brisé de tant d'angoisse tu auras à penser l'impensable' [If you don't die heart-broken from so much anguish you will have to think the unthinkable] (p. 274/p. 215). This 'unthinkable' decision to reject the necessity of violence and the inevitability of a deadly subjectivity is made possible, according to Cixous, by her close relationship with the political and writing practice of *des femmes*, and, in particular, with Antoinette Fouque. In an essay published at the end of the French text of *Angst*, Cixous celebrates her association with *des femmes*, saying that it has allowed her to confront the anguish and pain implicit in the identities she has inhabited, because it has offered her a glimpse of an alternative political and subjective economy which is available for women. Thus, in *Angst*, Cixous feels able to describe the anguish of her past, because she has rejected its inevitability for her future: she has looked god in the face and discovered he does not exist (p. 275/p. 215).

This individual subjective journey through separation and loss, and towards an alternative space of writing, also forms the basis of Cixous's *Préparatifs de noces au delà de l'abîme*.[17] The title of this novel echoes Kafka's *Wedding Preparations in the Country*: a story which dramatizes the subjective crises that beset a young man who is preparing for marriage. Kafka shows the fear of appropriation that dominates his hero's mind, and leads him to a desperate attempt to separate himself from the identity presupposed by his own actions:

> And so long as you can say 'one' instead of 'I', there's nothing in it and you can easily tell the story, but as soon as you admit to yourself that it is you yourself, you feel as though transfixed and are horrified.[18]

In Cixous's text the marriage under discussion is that between the woman narrator and the abyss. Having begun with a painful sense of isolation, and a fear of stepping out into the sterility that surrounds her, the narrator then undoes the meanings and symbols that led her to this state of paralysis. She comes to see the abyss as a necessary moment of confrontation that can lead her to the resources of her own subjectivity, and her own writing. The fear and deferral that haunt Kafka's hero are rejected in favour of joyful consummation of a marriage that eschews all naming other than the affirmation of 'you'.

In both of these texts the bisexuality dramatized in *La* has given way to a political and subjective identification with the shared struggle of women, and to an assertion of the resources implicit in the feminine libidinal economy. This move is confirmed in the structure and imagery of Cixous's novel *Illa*. *Illa* is a novel in three parts: the first exploring separation, the second proposing the possibility of Illa's liberation, and the third specifying the power of Lispector's writing as a metaphor for women's struggle.

'Illa' is the feminine form of the demonstrative in Latin: as a pronoun, although it can simply mean 'she', it can also carry connotations of 'that one there' or 'that one you know of'.[19] Both of these meanings are explored in this novel which sets out to describe the absent woman, and to consider the pleasures and the pitfalls of recognition. 'Illa' is also the first word of a passage from Virgil's *Georgics* which Cixous cites, which deals with the story of Orpheus' failed attempt to rescue Eurydice from the underworld. Despite clear instructions, Orpheus looks back at Eurydice, and negates forever the possibility of her escape. Eurydice, understandably angry, protests:

Then thus the bride: 'what fury seized on thee,
Unhappy man! to lose thyself and me?'[20]

In *Illa* Eurydice's fate is contrasted with the story of Demeter
and Persephone (also referred to as Koré), where Demeter's
loyalty in the face of Persephone's abduction becomes a figure
of the ways in which women can challenge the loss and separation of the Orphic myth.

Although in *La* the underworld seemed to be a space of
transformation, in *Illa* it is associated with death and loss.
Demeter's refusal to accept the inevitability of Persephone's
disappearance thus becomes a powerful challenge to the dominant subjective economy which tends to internalize fear and
to recognize self only in relation to an absent Other. Demeter's
insistent search for her missing daughter thus becomes a metaphor for Cixous's own persistent search for a feminine identity
which would not be overdetermined by the voice of the man
who is more *'fort'* than *'da'* (p. 111). Koré's status as desired
other woman is used by Cixous to generate a whole series of
associations with 'corps' and 'cœur' [body and heart], as well
as with Shakespeare's Cordelia, who refused to produce herself as demanded by the dominant discourse of her father, and
opted instead for silence.

These stories of mythic couples are constantly disrupted by
the imagery of *Illa*, which refuses duality. A third term always
intervenes to break up the security of dualist thought, with
images of the triple identity of women, as maidens, mothers,
or crones, of their three libidos, of the garden which is three
times as green, of 'la troisième' which can be understood as
writing, as the nature of 'Illa', as the role of Cixous as author,
or as an attempt to invert the classic trinity based on the Father
and the Son by invoking the relationship between mother and
daughter.

The imprisonment of the underworld and the obliteration
implicit in the Orphic myth are explored through a range of
intertextual references. The 'casket scene' in *The Merchant of
Venice* becomes a classic representation of the structures of
patriarchal kinship, where the marriage partner is chosen on
the basis of his structural similarity to the bride's father rather
than any relationship with the bride (p. 38). The ultimate
redundancy and structural overdetermination of this choice

between three caskets is then contrasted with the substantial choice that faces women in this novel: the choice between two destinies, two doors, two libidinal economies (p. 62).

The use of myth in *Illa* is markedly different from its use in *La*, and arguably less successful. In *La* Cixous seems to exploit the ambiguity of mythic narrative: realizing that it could not but be complicit with the dominant culture, she none the less rewrites it in ways that facilitate the exploration of its blind-spots and move beyond its categorical oppositions. In *La* her mythic allusions combine seriousness with humour, and fascination with scepticism, in a way that supports the innovations of her political and subjective vision. In *Illa*, however, the uses of myth seem to rely much more heavily on its referential, than on its associative, meanings. The story of Demeter and Persephone is mobilized as feminist heroic narrative, in a way that begs precisely the kinds of questions about knowledge and power that are so important to Cixous's work as a whole.

This use of myth is clearly related to Cixous's confidence in her ability to conceive, and to realize in writing, an alternative social and sexual economy: a space where the repeated demands to identify the truth of woman's identity, or of homo-sexuality, would be displaced by the power of the fact of recognition. Many of her formulations in *Illa* are compelling, with their suggestion of an intersubjective identity which moves beyond the dilemma of separation, of presence and absence:

> Si en moi Cordelia reprend souffle après que j'aie expiré sur ses lèvres c'est qu'une femme m'a entendue me taire en Cordelia, et a respiré pour moi quand j'étouffais.
>
> (p. 83)

> [If Cordelia starts to breathe again in me after I have expired on her lips, it is because a woman heard me become silent in Cordelia, and breathed for me when I was suffocating.]

The celebratory tone of the novel offers the woman reader a sense of recognition, and the experience of reading 'une femme s'adressant en chair et en chant à une elle' [a woman address-ing, in the flesh and in song, another she] offers its own pleasures (p. 12). Overall, however, there is a sense of difficulties avoided, and complexity repressed, due to the urgency of the project of delivering Illa from her deadly fate.

The role of Lispector is crucial to this liberation of Illa: Lispector's writing becomes the third term for which the narrator was seeking. Much of the imagery and argument about Lispector is already familiar from *Vivre l'orange*: she offers a new way of approaching the other, a reassessment of ethical and aesthetic hierarchies – 'la voix-Clarice. Elle donne un boire à Illa, la troisième, depuis des mois' [the voice of Clarice. She has been offering refreshment to *Illa*, the third one, for months] (p. 131). Once again, Lispector offers the possibility of a mutual recognition that would facilitate women's struggle to establish different modes of writing, and different ways of relating to each other: 'l'orange entre comme un oiseau par la fenêtre de ma poitrine' [the orange enters like a bird through the window in my breast] (p. 148). In *Illa*, Lispector also offers a point of resistance to the apparent drift towards mass culture with its mechanized and reductive processes of thought, by her careful use of language and her respect for the specificity of each separate thing. Moving beyond the disruptive knowledges of Nietzsche's *The Gay Science*, Lispector's writing offers instead the possibility of 'Gay Ignorance', a form of writing that would escape the dead weight of categorization and established knowledges (p. 211).

As in *Vivre l'orange*, much of Cixous's writing about Lispector in *Illa* is both exciting and original. In the overall structure of the novel, however, its status is problematic, since it seems to require a narrator who is a much more univocal presence than is suggested by the mythic intertextuality of the first half of the novel. *Illa* still contains traces of Cixous's interest in processes of division, in subjective complexity, and in the power of the unconscious, yet it also seems to strain towards the relative security of a new form of identity. The tension between the recognition of difference and the need for identity is indeed part of the story of *Illa*, but its resolution at the level of narrative voice is often uneasy. As Cixous says: 'il est étrangement difficile de parler des femmes auxquelles nous touchons, qui nous touchent' [it is strangely difficult to speak about the women we are in contact with, who touch us] (p. 117), and the difficulties remain throughout the text of *Illa*. The possibility of a politicized feminine identity, which both recognizes the

95

complexities of subjectivity and exploits the potential of mythic narrative for a re-conceptualization of social and subjective relations, has to wait for Cixous's later novel *Le Livre de Promethea*.

Le Livre de Promethea is a powerful and fascinating text, which dramatizes the possibility of a relationship of intersubjective identification that is not a relationship of negation and death.[21] Subjective divisions are no longer a source of anguish in this text, but rather the means through which to realize the necessary alliances and contradictions implicit in living a feminine identity. In dividing the action of this novel between three characters, and placing them in a productive intertext of mythical allusion, Cixous is able to explore the implications and limitations of different subjective identities, and to suggest the sustainability of a relationship whose intensity moves it beyond the Law.

At the beginning of this novel we are introduced by the narrator to 'H' and to Promethea. H is an old ally in writing. In this instance, however, she is unable to tell the narrator how to begin, and can reach no level of articulacy beyond a kind of humming. H is preoccupied with settling old intellectual accounts. She had been struggling for years to find in theoretical discourses the means to understand the world, but had now concluded that they were simply so many illusions, which lacked the 'lightness' necessary to productive knowledge. H looks over her beautiful theories from 'celle de la bisexualité qui me donna toujours un peu de mal' [the theory of bisexuality which always gave me a little difficulty], to her later interest in Rossini and Tasso, but concludes that they are all getting in the way of her attempt to understand subjectivity and pleasure (p. 13). The echo of Cixous's own theoretical explorations is, of course unmistakable, yet H cannot be identified simply with Cixous's past: she has a fictional autonomy that precludes such a reductive analysis.

Promethea, as her name suggests, embodies the Promethean predisposition towards trangression, and also has the capacity to produce fire, of a creative and erotic nature. Cixous's use of the myth of Prometheus owes a lot to Shelley, for whom Prometheus was a symbol of creative striving, which tyrannical authority sought in vain to repress.[22] The feminization of such creative energy in the figure of Promethea is a crucial element of her strength, an element which she is able to celebrate without anguish: 'jamais Promethea n'a pensé à dire: "je suis une femme." (Et cependant elle l'est)' [Promethea has never thought to say: 'I am a woman.' (And yet she is one)] (p. 15). Promethea is the narrator's lover and her Other, and constantly challenges her to risk more, to challenge the inevitability of the laws and the gods to which she submits herself.

The relationship between these three women is fundamentally linked to the structure and the imagery of *Le Livre de Promethea*. The narrator's aim is to write herself into a relation of proximity 'jusqu'à pouvoir épouser le contour de leurs âmes avec la mienne, sans cependant causer de confusion' [to the point of being able to wed the outline of their souls to my own, without, however, causing any blurring] (p. 12). Such subjective complexity necessitates a fragmented text, where different sections sketch out the relationships between the different characters, and tentatively explore the implications of Promethea's creative and ethical vision. Thus *Le Livre de Promethea* consists of two notebooks, as well as a 'portrait' of Promethea, and various prefatory and linking sections.

The structural complexities of *Le Livre de Promethea* form part of the novel's theme. 'Je' asks both Promethea and H for advice, and wrestles with the form in which parts of the text come to her from them. The only structural model she can find for her writing is that of the prehistoric caves at Lascaux: a series of separate caves linked in an overall pattern, whose paintings demonstrate the fundamental human drive towards creativity. Promethea is unsure about the way in which the narrator is proceeding, and chides her for the device of splitting and doubling implicit in the use of 'H' and 'je'. Promethea also challenges the veracity of the narrator's description of her relationship with the other characters:

> Elle a lu, elle est devenue triste devant mes yeux, heur-
> eusement! Sinon j'aurais continué honteusement, peur-
> eusement, secrètement à me dérober. Et tristement, elle
> a murmuré: 'tu n'as pas écrit que je t'aime'.
>
> (p. 28)

> [She read, she became sad in front of my eyes, happily!
> If she had not I would have continued to shy away,

shamefully, fearfully, secretly. And sadly, she murmured:
'you have not written that I love you'.]

Such intervention serves further to complicate the authority of
the writing in this text, since even the voice of 'je' cannot be
read as completely reliable, as free of the evasions and fears
that get in the way of the realization of an alternative subjective
and sexual economy.

The inadequacies of language were an important theme for
Cixous at this point, as has been demonstrated in relation to
both 'Tancredi Continues' and 'Le dernier tableau ou le portrait
de dieu'. These linguistic explorations of the limits of language
produce many stylistic innovations, and a series of attempts
to move beyond the fixity and subjective eradication Cixous
sees as the constant risk of language. The narrator attempts
to paint a portrait of Promethea, but realizes that she must
have her eyes closed in order to avoid the violence of specular-
ity. She also stresses that the sense of touch is the most important resource for such a project. Throughout the novel, the
narrator struggles to invent new linguistic forms and novelistic
structures that could capture the originality of Promethea as
heroine:

Promethea est mon héroïne.
Mais la question de l'écriture est mon adversaire.

(p. 21)

[Promethea is my heroine.
But the question of writing is my adversary.]

This interrogation of the limits of language produces an amus-
ing ironic distance between the narrator and her text, as she
draws attention to the way that language produces, or at least
inflects, her identity: 'j'étais tombée au pouvoir d'une méta-
phore très maléfique' [I had fallen under the influence of a
metaphor with very evil powers'] (p. 105). The narrator constantly reflects on, and reshapes, the imagery she brings to
the text. She expresses her frustration that she is unable to
capture in language the beauty she is trying to describe. Only
Promethea seems to have moved beyond the paralysis of
linguistic structures, as she has of sexual structures, since 'Promethea est la personne qui n'a pas coupé le cordon qui relie

la parole à son corps' [Promethea is the person who has not cut the cord which links speech to her body] (p. 184).

Promethea, indeed, is exemplary. She lives the implications of the revolutionary changes embodied in the concept of a feminine economy, and has chosen

> entre deux conceptions de l'amour, de la vie, deux versions des mystères essentiels, deux manières de penser la présence des créatures sur cette terre, deux philosophies, en somme, deux façons d'évaluer la bonté, la justice, le droit, la liberté.
>
> (p. 152)

> [between two conceptions of love, of life, two versions of the essential mysteries, two ways of thinking about the presence of creatures on this earth, two philosophies, in short, two manners of evaluating goodness, justice, right, liberty.]

She transforms herself into many different creatures, a horse, a doe, a lioness, an eagle, in order to explore the dimensions of her being. She gallops through the forest, with her mane flying, leaving the narrator both exhilarated and terrified from trying to run beside such a powerful beast. Promethea embodies many of the values Cixous found in Lispector's writing: innocence, simplicity, nudity. Yet she combines these with an energy, and a propensity towards excess and violence, which relate her rather to Cixous's earlier heroine: Penthesilea.

Promethea also has a revolutionary relationship to death: she admits it into her life, rather than repressing it, 'Promethea en parle beaucoup, imprudemment, sans pudeur, avec familiarité' [Promethea speaks about it a lot, imprudently, without modesty, with familiarity] (p. 153). She even lends the narrator her death and asks her to look after it for her. The scandalousness of this attitude provokes the narrator to question the fear and repression of death that have dominated her life, and to risk the integrity of herself in an all-consuming relationship with Promethea.

The risk of death, and its relation to writing, recurs in *Le Livre de Promethea* in the form of allusions to the stories of *The Arabian Nights*. To some extent, the point of these allusions is to suggest a literary domain of fantasy, whose exoticism places it outside the dominant narrative and ethical structures of western literary texts. The massive popularity of these tales in Europe in the nineteenth century does, however, tend to diminish the effectiveness of such claims for their 'otherness'. Yet we can never forget that these stories were originally told in order to avoid death: Scheherazade struggling to deflect her husband's murderous intent by entrancing him with her fantastic tales. They thus invite speculation on the narrator's intentions in telling her stories, speculation that is reinforced by her admission that she could kill Promethea if she were to write the wrong sentence.

Relations between violence and consuming love are intimate throughout *Le Livre de Promethea*. Total identification with an Other threatens the subject with annihilation, while separation leads to unbearable grief. The tension between these two options, and the struggle to move beyond them, result in a series of images of cannibalism and mutual eradication. Yet such moments are never without hope: the narrator learns that what she had seen as a terrifying dependence might be better understood as 'generosity'; the figure of H is constantly ready to intervene in order to break up the potentially destructive couple; the ontological status of the conflict is put in doubt by the text's self-referentiality. Finally, Promethea has an impressive sense of timing, and interrupts to suggest defrosting the fridge, or offers to cook some fried eggs at moments of crisis. The effect of this intrusion of the domestic is not, as it might be, banal. Rather, it increases the ironical distance between the narrator and her text, while setting up structures of recognition that add significantly to the undoubted charm of this novel.

In *Le Livre de Promethea*, Cixous succeeds in creating a novel that dramatizes many of her convictions about the transformative potential of a feminine economy. Her allusive use of myth facilitates this process, since it allows her to call on the resources of the dominant culture without being trapped within it. Milton, Dante, Shelley, Ariosto, and the Bible offer her narratives and images which she combines within a collage of voices that subvert their authority while acknowledging their intellectual and emotional power. The structural and technical problems inherent in organizing such a range of allusions into a fictional text are discussed throughout *Le Livre de Promethea*, where the narrator makes it clear that any ending to the fiction will necessarily be arbitrary, will do some kind of violence to 'Je', H, and Promethea. The power of this observation is suggested by the fact that Cixous went on to pursue the adventures of Promethea and H in *La Bataille d'Arcachon*. All texts must end somewhere, however, and *Le Livre de Promethea* concludes with a humour and a linguistic economy worthy of Promethea herself:

> –Ah j'ai oublié!: Promethea tombe amoureuse.
> –Tombe?
> –Est. (p. 248)

> [–Ah I forgot!: Promethea falls in love.
> –Falls?
> –Is.]

Cixous's recent novel, *Manne* [Manna], is also concerned with the social implications of sustaining an oppositional subjective and ethical economy. This fictional text is based on the lives of Winnie and Nelson Mandela and of Osip and Nadezhda Mandelshtam, which it uses as the bases of a mythical exploration of the power of individual and collective resistance. Various episodes from the lives of all four characters provide the structure for this fictional exploration, which attempts to find a form to move beyond the contingencies of contemporary history towards the more universal narratives of myth.

This fictional text clearly owes much to Cixous's recent theatrical writings, which will be discussed in the next chapter. The fact that some of the material from this book is being reworked by Cixous for her next play, *Voile noire, voile blanche* [Black Sail, White Sail], suggests the extent to which the project is related to her theatrical explorations of recent history. In its analysis of the transformative capacity of a relationship of love, however, it can also be related to both *Le Livre de Promethea* and *La Bataille d'Arcachon*.

The juxtaposition of the Mandelas and the Mandelshtams, despite the similarity of names, is at first surprising. What can South African freedom fighters have in common with a poet from the Soviet Union, who was persecuted and eventually killed by Stalin, and the wife who preserved his late poems? For Cixous, the answer lies not in the details of their lives, but in the extent to which they all refused to submit to a brutal and morally corrupt authority. She weaves the lives of these four characters into her text, producing an imagery of flight, aspiration, and resistance that unites all four characters in an epic and heroic struggle. Cixous declares:

> Ce livre voudrait être une déclaration d'amour . . . à tous les donneurs de feu qui payent de leurs ailes pour que les humains voient un peu plus clair dans le noir . . . Ce livre est une tentative de compassion.
>
> (pp. 13 and 25)

> [This book aims to be a declaration of love . . . for all the fire-givers who pay with their wings for human beings to be able to see a little more clearly in the darkness . . . This book is an attempt at compassion.]

Cixous's interest in individuals who move outside the Law goes back a long way, and can be seen in her discussions of Kafka, or of Kleist's 'Michael Kohlhaas'. It had already led her to intervene in contemporary political struggle as early as 1975, when she published a defence of Pierre Goldman, a Polish Jew who had been convicted of 'being capable' of carrying out a hold-up.[23] Cixous wrote of Goldman as a figure of resistance to the homogenization of modernity, an outsider who opened a crack in the system. It is as such an outsider that she represents Osip Mandelshtam.

Mandelshtam's eccentricity lay in his commitment to cultural tradition at a time of revolutionary innovation. Convinced that 'on a beau dire que l'amour a des ailes, le siècle les a plumées' [it is vain to say that love has wings, this century has plucked them], he turned to Classicism, to Petrarch and to Dante, in order to find a poetic tradition that would speak beyond the priorities of the contemporary moment (p. 140). His belief in the sustainability of such a tradition broke down in the late 1920s, when he stopped writing poetry and turned to prose. What interests Cixous, however, is his reasons for returning to poetry at a time when the social and political stakes in doing so were so high. That he also wrote a satirical poem on Stalin sealed his fate, which was to die of starvation in a prison camp after years of exile.

Cixous explores the meaning of such a dangerous commitment to the poetic, which led Mandelshtam to carry on writing in exile and in the prison camp. It was clearly destructive of both himself and his family: his wife travels with him into exile, and spends years of her life in an unsuccessful attempt to discover the precise details of his death.[24] Yet, *Manne* suggests, this was not wasted time. Eventually, Nadezhda recognizes that the only truth she can discover is that there is no truth: the 'witness' to her husband's death has lost his memory. She is left discussing the implications of this with the poet Anna Akhmatova, and wondering about the power of his poetic legacy: 'Si l'on savait. . . . ce qu'est un poète? Peut-être ses poèmes? Peut-être ces ossements qui vivent obstinément' [If one knew . . . what a poet is? Perhaps his poems? Perhaps these bones which obstinately live] (p. 340).

The conflict between individual need and social commitment is also explored in the sections of the novel dealing with the Mandelas, where we see the intensity of an erotic and loving relationship forced into the margins by the priorities of political struggle. We are shown their first meeting, the beginnings of their love, and the early years of their married life. The terms in which these are represented, however, demonstrate some of the problems with Cixous's attempt to move from history to myth. The mythical imagery that already surrounds Nelson Mandela is just much more extensive than that which is available for Winnie. Nelson becomes 'a planet, a temple, a mountain', while Winnie is a 'doe' or an 'ant'. From *Le Livre de Promethea* we know that Cixous sees the doe as a powerful image of the grace and beauty of the feminine. Yet, when applied to a contemporary historical figure, such imagery has meanings that cannot be confined to the intense personal imagery of Cixous's texts.

Cixous frequently risks reproducing a version of Winnie as the patient, passive, and silent woman, whose identity has no significance apart from her relationship with Nelson. At times, indeed, she sees such self-obliteration as part of the power of Winnie, which allows her to sustain the loss and separation of so many years. Again, there are echoes of *Promethea* in this intense erotic intersubjective relation, but when applied to a relationship between a man and a woman, who live within the structures of contemporary political struggle, such representations can only be uncomfortable in their familiarity.

Cixous does also try to find narratives that will embody Winnie's strength and courage. Thus we hear of the wedding cake which Winnie and Nelson did not have time to eat, but which Winnie preserves through all the years of harassment and brutality as a symbol of survival. We follow her work with black women in the townships and in her enforced exile, her attempts to politicize and to improve their material living conditions. This conscious political struggle, however, sits in an uneasy relationship with the imagery that surrounds Winnie as African mother. Cixous uses Winnie's African name, Zami, in order to suggests the complexity of her identity as one caught between tribal relations and the political structures of modernity. The version of her African identity we are offered, however, seems to reinforce many myths that serve to place Africa 'outside' the political space of the contemporary, and to associate it with the mysterious, the ancient, and the natural.

Despite these difficulties, *Manne* is a courageous text. Such public identification by a writer with the armed struggle of the ANC is far from usual. The implications of such a commitment, however, remain unclear, precisely because of the strong parallel Cixous draws between the Mandelas and the Mandelshtams as figures of resistance. Writing poetry and waging a guerrilla war are not the same, yet *Manne* deals with both at a level of abstraction that renders such distinction almost irrelevant.[25] We are thus left with a slight feeling that some important questions have been evaded by the sheer virtuosity of Cixous's metaphorical associations.

Such virtuosity is apparent throughout the text, whose imagery offers both surprising and powerful recognitions. Thus Cixous begins with a dedication to the ostrich, whose loss of flight is represented as a punishment for the power of its creative energy. She introduces a dramatic interlude in which a crocodile hunts an antelope, only to be chased off by a hippopotamus: an episode which represents the power of resistance, even from the most unlikely quarters. Likewise, we hear of the anonymous woman who throws a sweet through the train window as the Mandelshtams travel into exile, risking her own freedom in order to offer them some hope. As these brief episodes build up, so does the power of the structure of resistance Cixous sets out to create, so that by the end of the text we too are ready to believe in the relevance and importance of maintaining 'hope against hope', and prepared to receive: 'la manne. La manne venue du ciel caché sous la terre. Elle a un goût de nécessité' [manna. Manna which comes from the heavens which are hidden under the earth. It has a flavour of necessity] (p. 325).

The ambiguity surrounding the status of this text, however, remains: if it is a fiction, to what extent does its factual accuracy matter? If it is a history, can it also, productively, be a myth? Can the emotional power of a mythic text be the means of transforming our historical knowledge, or does it simply supplement or refine it? In order to assess the implications of such questions for Cixous's work, I will now turn to her work for the theatre, where the negotiations between contemporary history and theatrical form allow us to see more clearly both the strengths and the limitations of creating a mythology for the contemporary world.

4

STAGING HISTORY

Pour commencer, prenons le Théâtre au sérieux
('Le lieu du crime', p. 259)

Much of Cixous's recent writing has been for, or concerned with, the theatre. Theatre has provided Cixous with a space in which to develop her analyses of subjectivity, to explore further the bodily roots of meaning, to challenge what she sees as the dominant forms of thought and reason, and to posit new structures of historical explanation. Increasingly frustrated by the cultural embeddedness of language, Cixous has moved to the theatre as a space where the poetic can still survive within the forms of a public and accessible ritual.

Theatre's specificity lies in its organization of both space and time. The importance of spatial metaphor to Cixous's writing project has already been noted: she frequently uses spatial relations to represent so-far unrealized conceptual or political relations. The attraction of a medium that can give concrete form to such spatialized thought is clear, and Cixous, in collaboration with a number of different directors, uses the spatial dimensions of theatre in quite conscious and transgressive ways, in order to open up multiple points of view, to complicate the relations between language and character, and to provide a framework for the mythic narratives she wishes to develop in her historical dramas.

The temporal dimension of theatre can be related to Cixous's interest in forms of thought that do not rely on hierarchies of opposition, but are instead open to the possibility of multiple differences. Such forms of thought are theorized by Derrida under the sign of '*différance*', a term which aims to capture the structural and temporal dimensions of meaning, understood as processes of differing and deferring. Derrida describes the process of *différance* as 'the becoming-time of space and the becoming-space of time', and asks, '*Différance* as temporization, *différance* as spacing. How are they to be joined?'[1] The importance of philosophical categories that avoid abstract equivalences or categorical oppositions in favour of a never completely finished process of production of meaning is thus related to the importance of thinking along both spatial and temporal axes: the axes that structure theatrical performance.

The temporal dimension of theatre also returns Cixous to the thought of Heidegger, who stressed the ways in which a recognition of the temporal aspects of Being lead to the confrontation of our own mortality, and thus to the necessity of choice. As Cixous says,

> Je vais au théâtre parce que j'ai besoin de comprendre ou au moins de contempler l'acte de la mort, ou au moins de l'admettre, de le méditer.

> [I go to the theatre because I need to understand, or at least to contemplate, the act of death, or at least to accept it, to meditate upon it.][2]

Cixous stresses the importance for theatre of moments of crisis, of personal or historical turning points, which carry within them the possibility of change. She also stresses the sense of anticipation which accompanies a theatrical production. Unlike a novel, time cannot be re-run, the ending cannot be read first. The audience is locked into the bodily experience of time, and 'avance le cœur battant de ne pas savoir ce qui va arriver' [moves forward with a heart which is beating from not knowing what is going to happen next].[3]

The intensity of Cixous's evocation of the opacity of the temporal in theatrical representation seems to be related to some sort of conviction about the specificity and non-reproducibility of any given performance of a play: the idea that theatre is necessarily both here and now. This conviction is reminiscent of Antonin Artaud's attempt to develop the theoretical and theatrical bases of his 'theatre of cruelty' in ways that would divorce it from the tyranny of the text and the threat of repetition. Derrida has analysed Artaud's writings about theatre in ways that point up the philosophical stakes of such theatrical practice. Derrida sees Artaud as struggling to achieve 'the inaccessible limit of a representation which is not repetition, of a representation which is full presence, which does not carry its double within itself as its death'.[4] In this project, Derrida argues, Artaud is bound to fail, but the effort at least shows up the structure of repetition that underlies representation, and reveals the limits of the linguistic dependency that defines most contemporary Western theatre. As Artaud himself says, 'An actor does not repeat the same gestures twice, but he gesticulates, moves, and although he brutalises forms, as he destroys them he is united with what lives on behind and after them, producing their continuation'.[5]

The struggle to escape from reproduction, and from repetition, dominates Cixous's writings on theatre, and can be related to her critique of the cultural and political effects of mass culture. In the theatre, she argues, we can regain much that we have lost, including:

> l'espoir que les choses, qui nous servent d'Histoire et d'existence, et qui sont si implacablement programmées par les grandes machines sociales, échappent à toute prévision; et s'offrent à la chance, à l'humain.
>
> ('Le chemin', p. 9)

> [the hope that the things which stand as History and as existence for us, and which are so implacably programmed by the great social machinery, will escape from all prior expectation, and offer themselves to chance, to the human.]

Regaining the weight of the present moment is, for Cixous, a way of rejecting the inevitability of the social structures that we inhabit. It is also related to the complicated experience of the bodily, which Cixous opposes to the superficiality and externality of mass-produced cultural forms ('Le lieu du crime', p. 254). Here again, the echo of Artaud is palpable, since he it was who said that 'to make speech or verbal expression dominant over the objective expressiveness of gestures and everything on stage spatially affecting the mind through the senses, means turning our backs on the physical requirements of the stage and rebelling against its potential'.[6]

Theatre thus, for both Cixous and Artaud, is crucially bound up with the temporal and the bodily. It is a form in which it is possible to challenge the inevitable dominance of the linguistic, and to posit meanings that are not bound up with repetition, stereotype, or the security of 'character'. The weight that the form must carry in Cixous's writing is thus considerable. Not only does it have to contribute to the modernist rejection of mass culture, and the consequent opening-up of language and subjectivity, but it also has to provide an alternative cultural sphere to that of the post-modern with its stress on image, superficiality, and repetition.

The stakes are high, and they sometimes lead Cixous to forms of abstraction, or of unfocused optimism, which have provoked some rather bad-tempered responses from those who look to her to provide a consistently deconstructive reading of phallogocentrism.[7] Yet Cixous's writing on the theatre, as on other things, is always strategic. She uses the theatrical as a space in which to develop her critique of the forms of subjectivity and representation that dominate contemporary life. She does not assume that theatre is immune from the gender, economic, and political pressures that structure modernity, but she does argue for it as a site in which the inevitability of these pressures can be challenged. To do so, as she is well aware, requires substantial theoretical and theatrical work, as well as a commitment to the potential of theatre as a form. All of these are exhibited in Cixous's brief, but telling, statement on the problematic relation of women to the practices of contemporary theatre, 'Aller à la mer'.[8]

This short essay, written in 1977, begins with a consideration of the problematic relation of women to the theatre: a space in which they have been consistently objectified and turned into victims. Referring to the ultimate fate of Electra, of Ophelia, and of Cordelia, Cixous concludes that theatre functions as specular fantasy, where women characters function as mirrors of male heroism. Women in such theatre are in the space of the silenced and the repressed, their bodies both negated and elevated to the level of display.[9]

Cixous completely rejects such voyeuristic theatre, yet remains committed to the potential of the form: 'If I go to the theatre now it must be a political gesture, with a view to changing, with the help of other women, its means of production and expression' (p. 547). Such transformations would involve breaking down the fixity of theatrical space and point of view, moving away from specular illusion to stress the bodily presence of actors on the stage. Character, as a fixed and stable location of theatrical meanings, would also have to be challenged by a theatrical form that was not afraid to explore subjectivity and its relation to the unconscious. Finally, in a modification of the Brechtian position, Cixous argues that such political theatre would have to emphasize proximity, involvement, rather than the distance that supports an illusion of unity and coherence for most dramatic performance. Only if these issues are addressed, Cixous argues, will women feel themselves comfortable in, welcomed by, part of, the cultural space of theatre.

Yet Cixous remains convinced of the importance of theatre as a cultural space. Firstly, it is a cultural form which can only function dialogically, there is no theatre without an audience:

> Le théâtre c'est le palais d'autrui. Il vit du désir de l'autre, de tous les autres. Et du désir du désir des autres: du public, des comédiens.

> [Theatre is the palace of other people. It lives on the desire of the other, and of all others. And on the desire for the desire of others: of the public, of the actors.][10]

Secondly, it is a cultural form with an historically identifiable social role, whose collective nature Cixous finds both compelling and disturbing:

> Mais je déclare que nous avons besoin de ces temples sans dogme et sans doctrine (mais non sans un grand nombre de dieux) où se jouent nos affres et surtout nos aveuglements.
>
> ('Le lieu', p. 256)

> [But I declare that we need these temples without dogma and without doctrine (but not without a great many gods) where our torments, and particularly our blindnesses, are played out.]

In this project, Cixous's influences are diverse. From Shakespeare she borrows the conception of a relation between the psychological complexities of an individual and objective historical forces. From Greek tragedy she derives an enormity of vision, a capacity for the mythic. From Italian opera she learns the possibility of using the stage as a space of gender transgression, of suspension of categorization. Finally, from Artaud, Brecht, Beckett, and the Théâtre du Soleil she gains the resources to develop a theatrical form that can explore cultural and gender difference, while staging individual and social history in a way that opens itself to the mythic and the cultural and ethical Other.

Cixous's earliest dramatic text is *La Pupille,* an adaptation of elements of her novel, *Révolutions pour plus d'un Faust. La Pupille* was published in 1971, but never performed. This text is interesting, both for the ways in which it prefigures images and problematics which will be developed in later plays, and for its excess which renders it unperformable. In this play, Cixous has begun to think about the dramatic potential of the conflicts with which she is engaged, but has not yet developed a sense of the scale and structure of text that can work in a theatrical context.

The play involves the journey of two characters, the Fool and the Subject, who are figuratively represented by the eye and the pupil, but who are also supposed to represent Virgil and Dante in their journey through Hell. The play is organized round the exploration of three scenes of barbarism: the massacre of Vietnamese civilians by US soldiers at My Lai; political oppression and violence in contemporary Brazil; and the treatment of the Communards in nineteenth-century Paris. The influence of the events of 1968 is clear in this play which explores the festive element in popular struggle, setting it against the consistency of violence and oppression. The action of the play is divided into a large number of short episodes, including the entry of Death as a head with no body, which consumes itself; the appearance of Money who urges all those in power to serve his interests; and an elaborate parade of police brutality which articulates themes of separation, death, and instrumental rationality. Even Faust and Helen put in a brief appearance, borrowed briefly from Goethe's play.

The intertext of this play seems to be that of literary modernism, rather than any particular dramatic theory or writing. There is a very Joycean episode of masturbation and mirroring.

111

The metaphor of the eye, which recurs in both the staging and the action of the play, calls to mind Bataille's scandalous surrealist text, *The Story of the Eye*. Cixous uses the excesses, and the subjective and linguistic complexities, of these texts as the basis for beginning her exploration of the resources of theatre as a cultural medium.

The Maoist invocation of the transformative power of the labours of Chinese peasants in *La Pupille* now seems curiously dated, but the more general remark made by the voice of Theatre, that 'History comes from the East' relates interestingly to Cixous's later interest in cultures of the East as sites of resistance to the dominance of hierarchical and dualist thought.[11] The ambition of this text, its attempt to represent contemporary social forces and struggles, also prefigures the work that Cixous will do over ten years later with the Théâtre du Soleil. Finally, the attempt to represent the disruptive and transgressive potential of desire as a social force relates very closely to the earliest of Cixous's plays to be successfully performed: *Portrait de Dora*.

Portrait of Dora was written as a result of Cixous's continuing engagement with the Freud text which had been so important to the structure and imagery of *Portrait du soleil*: the 'Dora' Case History. The play was originally written for radio, but was extensively reworked for the Théâtre d'Orsay production of 1976, directed by Simone Benmussa.[12]

The 'Dora' Case History has intrigued many feminist critics, writers, and film-makers over the last twenty years. Some have protested against the arrogance of Freud's interpretations of hysteria, others have focused on the ways in which novelistic devices structure and inflect Freud's 'scientific' discourse, yet others have concentrated on what Freud does not see, or misses out.[13] Although Cixous addresses all of these issues in her play, its main focus is the presentation of the disruptive potential of feminine subjectivity and the female body for the familial structures of patriarchy, and for the specular relations of theatre.

Cixous's aim in this play is to dramatize the energies and forces that lie behind Dora's hysteria, and to relate them to the circuits of exchange and desire so tantalizingly sketched out by Freud. Her aim is not to provide 'the truth' about Dora, or even to offer Dora as feminist heroine, but rather to open out the network of relations in which Dora is caught, and to assess the disruptive potential of Dora's refusal to assent to their reproduction. She also aims to use Dora as emblematic of a refusal to assent to the inevitability of a given economy of exchange, and to explore the implications of such refusal for the structures of mimetic representation.

From Freud, Cixous derives the possibility of seeing character not as something finished, the key to all actions, but rather as something structural and intersubjective. Dora is positioned within a circuit of desire and exchange, where individual character emerges as secondary to the compulsion of structure. Thus Herr K. propositions Dora with the remark that 'you know that my wife means nothing to me', the same phrase he used when seducing the Governess. Dora recognizes that she is being placed within a series of substitutions which make of her a desirable object, but she also realizes that in taking up the place assigned to her as woman she risks, like Herr K.'s wife, becoming nothing. Such repetitions and substitutions abound in the play, far more excessively than in Freud's text. Thus, Dora is 'like a mother' to Frau K.'s children, and threatens to take her place, or Dora dreams of making a phone call to Dr K., a composite version of Freud and Herr K. Such sliding characterizes the relations between different characters: it is often unclear to whom a particular remark is addressed, and characters split and multiply, with Freud at one point commenting on his own behaviour in the third person.

This subjective complexity is further emphasized by the staging, which sets up triangular relations between different sets of characters, and emphasizes the extent to which all the characters are caught up in a network, whose terms they seem doomed to reproduce. Even Freud is not exempt from this network, and Cixous stresses the ways in which he is involved in the various circuits of property and desire, allowing Dora to comment on his 'knowledge', his bodily presence, and his institutional power.

Benmussa's production stressed Cixous's exploration of subjective splitting and intersubjective circuits of exchange. Benmussa has described the action of the play as taking place across four different sorts of spaces: memory, the real, dream, and fantasy.[14] Each of these corresponded to a different form of representation: theatrical, novelistic, filmic, and choreographic. Thus Benmussa projected images of characters on different parts of the stage, either to complicate or to contradict the words being spoken on the stage. The seduction scene at the lake was filmed in a sequence directed by Marguerite Duras, and projected while Dora spoke of her reactions to it, her anger at its being described as 'imaginary', her anger at its having taken place. Balletic sequences were also used, to suggest the ritualistic and overdetermined nature of the movements and gestures of individual characters.

Benmussa was interested in directing *Portrait of Dora* precisely because of its potential for such explorations of subjectivity, desire, and the structures of theatrical representations. Benmussa has frequently chosen to adapt fictional texts for the theatre, feeling this allows her the necessary distance from the inevitability of the forms and practices of theatrical representation, and allows her to explore different possible relations between audience and stage. *Portrait of Dora*, as a triply mediated text, coming through Freud's text, Cixous's radio play, and *Portrait du soleil*, presented Benmussa with a text that was both 'strange' to theatre yet 'familiar' in its family dramas, and thus provided an important site for theoretical and practical exploration at the newly founded Actors' Workshop at the Théâtre d'Orsay. Like Cixous, Benmussa has expressed herself interested in the structures and power of the unconscious, and in a political theatre which would challenge 'the great edifying and reproducing machines that we see all around us at the moment' (*Benmussa Directs*, p. 11). What she aimed to achieve in the theatre, and with *Portrait of Dora*, was an opening-out of the very process of representation, a political challenge to the voyeuristic relations and narrative repetitions of most theatrical performances.

The originality and power of Cixous's engagement with the politics of theatrical representation has, however, been relatively little discussed. Instead, attention has tended to focus on the relation between Cixous's text and the original Case History. This is perhaps inevitable, given the importance of Freud's text for recent feminist analyses of female sexuality, but it has led to some exaggerated claims for the revolutionary and heroic status of the character of Dora in Cixous's play.

Such readings are clearly related to Cixous's remarks that

'Dora seemed to me to be the one who resists the system', or 'the hysteric is, to my eyes, the typical woman in all her force'. Yet it is important to remember that Cixous goes on to say, 'it is a force that was turned back against Dora'.[15] Certainly, Dora refuses to participate in the circuits of exchange that structure her familial situation. Unlike Frau K., she refuses to say 'it's impossible' to her lesbian desire, and she walks out on Freud in the middle of her treatment, provoking a violent and tormented response from Freud, who asks her finally to 'let me know what I'm doing' (p. 66). Dora 'jams' the smooth working of the adulterous and exploitative relations that surround her: her body obtrudes and forces a recognition of a subject position which is denied access to the symbolic. This disruption produces the excesses of mirroring, of duplication, of fragmentation, in the play. What it does not produce is any new ordering of subjective or social relations. Dora remains silenced, and answers Freud's amorous demand that she write to him by saying, 'Write? . . . That's not my affair', thus recognizing the limits of her own resistance (p. 66).

Cixous's Dora is compelling in her excess, in the extravagance of her dreams, and in her capacity to understand the patriarchal relations that structure her subjectivity, but she is not a revolutionary heroine. She is a damaged, silenced, and oppressed product of a murderous subjective and sexual economy, whose security Cixous can only trouble, whose demise she can only hint at.

Such theatrical exploration of the subjective structures of patriarchy was followed by the staging of Cixous's *L'Arrivante* at the Avignon Festival in 1977. This play was made up of a series of extracts from Cixous's novel, *La*, which explores the constitution and articulation of femininity as a function of complex and split subjectivity. The play was staged by Viviane Théophilidès, and involved the use of seven different actresses, whose words, gestures, and choreographed movements strove to represent the dynamic process of feminine subjectivity. Allusions to the mythic and the archaic were suggested by moments such as the opening of the play, where six of the actresses stood, one behind the other, in profile, suggesting the representational strategies of Egyptian art.[16]

The capacity of the mythic to figure the dynamic process of sexual differentiation was a crucial element in Cixous's next dramatic text, *Le Nom d'Œdipe* [The Name of Oedipus]. This text was part of a longer, unpublished, work entitled *Chant du corps interdit*. It was performed as an opera, with music by André Boucourechliev, at the Avignon Festival in 1978. The opera was staged in the round, using a bare black stage, decorated with pieces of differently coloured glass, and using projected images to enhance the symbolic universe of the performance. Much of Cixous's text was spoken rather than sung, with each character being represented both by a singer and an actor.

The naming of Oedipus in relation to sexual difference immediately evokes the figure of Freud, and the institution of psychoanalysis. However, it is not directly with Freud's texts that Cixous engages in this libretto, but, rather with Sophocles' *Oedipus the King*.[17] Of course, our sense of a post-Freudian Oedipal drama is bound to be present in any reading of this particular text, but it does not provide a key, or a master narrative.

Le Nom d'Œdipe explores many of the elements of Sophocles' drama, which it also opens out both structurally and dramatically, refusing the linear movement from ignorance to knowledge, minimizing the sense of quest. Much of the drama in Cixous's text is concentrated round questions of naming, rather than of knowing, round the relations between actions and their cultural representations. Here, Cixous is picking up on an element that is important, though often ignored, in Sophocles' text, an element that is expressed in Oedipus' final recognition that 'it's unfit to say what is unfit to do' (*Oedipus the King*, p. 171). Naming, in Cixous's text, is associated with the public, with the move from the eroticism of the intensity of mutual identification and exchange that characterizes Jocasta and Oedipus' relation, to the taboos and violence of the cultural.

The opera begins with Jocasta, represented by both singer and actor, begging Oedipus to renounce his name. Taking on the name, 'Oedipus', is here equated with public duty, with an obligation to the city of Thebes, and thus with the mechanisms of separation from Jocasta. Naming is also associated with origins, and with the confusion over origins which constitutes much of the tragedy of *Oedipus the King*. In Sophocles' play, Oedipus is searching for the origin of a curse on Thebes,

116

unaware that he himself is the source of that curse. Oedipus does not know his own family origins, does not know that the man he killed in anger was his father, Laius.

Cixous sees in this muddling of origins a potential source of transgression within the relations of patriarchy, a transgression whose enormity is clearly signalled in Sophocles' play. The refusal of the authority of origins characterizes the imaginary world where Cixous's Jocasta and Oedipus exchange names that are plural and fluid. Jocasta calls Oedipus her mother, as well as her lover and her son. Here naming escapes the hierarchy of oppositions and taboo. Yet Oedipus cannot, finally, resist the will to know, the desire to enter the world of cultural representations, to leave the imaginary world of his relation with Jocasta.

Jocasta's relation to naming is also quite ambiguous. She articulates her need for Oedipus as someone to whom she can murmur his names. Such plurality immediately challenges the possibility of singular identity, of fixed origins. Yet, at the same time, Jocasta is compelled by the power of naming, and thus reproduces herself as the woman 'before the Law'. She asks him, instead of saying 'Oedipus', simply to say 'I'. But this very articulation of selfhood involves a reference to hierarchical forms of discourse, a taking up of his place within language. Finally, Jocasta enters into the drama of naming with all of its implications. She fantasizes about naming as a means to avoid separation, though in fact it turns out to precipitate, to make final, just such separation. Jocasta remembers the silence, the sterility, she experienced on the death of her father, her conviction that had she been able to speak she would have avoided the final separation of death. (The echo of *Dedans* is sufficiently strong here to give weight to Cixous's remark that, in another historical period, she would have been Jocasta.[18]) Jocasta struggles to express herself, and her relation to Oedipus, outside the Law, telling Oedipus not to internalize fear. Yet she cannot resist the force of this Law. She asks Oedipus to say his name, so that she can stop dying, can be fixed in relation to him.[19] Such naming brings only separation and fear, and Jocasta's request that Oedipus offer her his name, his one single name, so that she will then agree to die, finally seems inevitable. Death is certainly to be her end in

117

this text which, like *Dora*, is a text of 'rebellion rather than revolution'.[20]

Oedipus enters, saying he has been lost 'among words and among the dead', that he is now ready to say his real name, that the old names are buried, that they can start all over again (pp. 81–2). But he is already too late: Jocasta is dead. Oedipus ends the opera singing and speaking of his horror, saying that he is no-one without Jocasta to tell him who he is, that she was his mother and his child, that his identification with her is so strong that he no longer knows who is dying. The audience, however, does not share his confusion, since Jocasta died on stage, while Oedipus is still alive, not even blinded.

The source of the tragedy in Cixous's text is complex, and made more so by Jocasta's seemingly willing participation in her own destruction. Jocasta's apparent assent to her own destruction makes it clear that *Le Nom d'Œdipe* has to be considered structurally, as a dramatization of the compulsion of particular theoretical and political structures, rather than as the tragedy of any individual character. The need for such a structural reading is emphasized not just by the splitting of different characters into different roles, but also by the temporal complexity of the opera, which makes it impossible to identify with the teleological progress of either Oedipus or Jocasta.

The action of *Le Nom d'Œdipe* begins in the middle of the narrative, with Jocasta begging Oedipus not to go to the city, not to try to undo the curse. Then we are returned to the beginnings of Jocasta and Oedipus' relation, which is characterized by plurality, mutual exchange, and lack of separation. As the opera progresses, the time-scale of the present, when Oedipus has assumed his name and his origin and has thus brought about Jocasta's destruction, is played against the past, against the imaginary of their relationship. The different actors playing both Jocasta and Oedipus dramatize these time-scales, as do the chorus, and the frequently present figure of Tiresias.

The dramatization of the struggle between past and present, between imaginary and symbolic, is overdetermined by the powerful compulsion of the Law. Only by the freezing of time could the Law be avoided, and this is impossible, particularly on the stage. The Chorus urges:

Ne dis pas les mots sinistres
Ne dis pas enfant, père, famille . . .
Ne dis plus les anciens mots
délicieux crache-les
Ce qui a été fait doit être effacé
Enseveli
Ensablé en silence.

(p. 57)

[Don't say the sinister words, don't say child, father,
family . . . Don't say the delicious old words any more,
spit them out. That which has been done should be
erased, buried, silted up by silence.]

But, as we have seen, such burial cannot be sustained, it is
always vulnerable to the action of the mole, or to the labours
of the archaeologist.

The impasse that dominates *Le Nom d'Œdipe*, the impossibility of avoiding names, is explicitly referred to the recognition
of sexual difference. At one point Jocasta and Oedipus seem
to reach a point of mutual recognition, but suddenly he asks,
'Why are you a woman?', and Jocasta becomes negated once
more (p. 71). Eventually they are both locked in silence. Jocasta
then begs Oedipus to name himself, to break the desert of
silence. Jocasta shouts his name and her love in a moment
that will lead to her death.

Neither Jocasta nor Oedipus can resist the symbolic: Jocasta
because she cannot sustain the weight of resistance, of freezing
time; Oedipus because his need for love, for self-constitution
through obliteration of the Other, exceeds what Jocasta can
give him. The insatiability of his deadly desire takes him out
towards the city, towards knowledge, towards his own origins,
and brings about Jocasta's destruction.

Le Nom d'Œdipe is a text which it is impossible to 'sum up'.
Its complex temporal structure and plurality of voices, both
spoken and sung, make any notion of character or of narrative
conclusion difficult to sustain. However, what can be said is
that it shifts the focus of Sophocles' text from the tragedy of
Oedipus to that of Jocasta, understood as typical of women's
exclusion from the symbolic. The opera also genders Oedipus'
search for knowledge and power, seeing them as manifestations of a particular form of subjectivity that can be consti-

tuted only through negation of the Other. Finally, however, it denies the possibility of recasting Jocasta as feminist heroine, leaving her instead as the point of resistance in a structure of symbolic and political violence.

The relations between resistance and violence are further explored in Cixous's next theatrical text, *La Prise de l'école de Madhubaï* [The Conquest of the School at Madhubai], which was first performed at the Petit Odéon in 1983.[21] This play represents an interesting point of transition in Cixous's theatrical writing. Like *Dora* and *Le Nom d'Œdipe*, it is principally concerned with women's relation to patriarchal culture. However, in its turning to the East, as a metaphorical site of values excluded by western modernity, and in its explicit exploration of political structures, it prefigures much of the work that Cixous will later produce with the Théâtre du Soleil.

La Prise de l'école de Madhubaï is a play involving only three characters. The heroine is an Indian guerrilla fighter called Sakundeva, who has spent years fleeing from the police, but has finally returned to her home village, and to her friend and mentor, Pandala. Their reunion is interrupted by the entry of the Minister, whose aim is to negotiate Sakundeva's surrender. The play charts the reasons for Sakundeva's decision to move beyond the law, in a series of discussions between Sakundeva and Pandala. Sakundeva, we learn, was abused as a child, and was then married off to an elderly and violent cousin. Seeing no alternative to a life of hardship and abuse, Sakundeva decided to flee from this domestic space, and became the leader of a gang which sought to redress the balance of power and wealth by direct, and violent, means. Such violence is treated as the only possible response to a structure of oppression that would otherwise have destroyed her. Like Kleist's Michael Kohlhaas, who was driven by an act of arbitrary tyranny to challenge the legitimacy of the State, Sakundeva's violence is laid at the door of an oppressive and patriarchal social structure.[22]

An alternative economy of social relations is suggested in the play by the relation between Pandala and Sakundeva. Pandala is an elderly woman, who has known Sakundeva since her childhood. She has the gift of second-sight, and has an intense bodily relation with Sakundeva. Thus, Sakundeva's arrival is predicted by Pandala, who imagines her successful flight from the police and her safe arrival home: 'My whole body is moved, as though I was awaiting Sakundeva' (p. 60). The intense physicality of the relationship is, however, referred to a hierarchy: Pandala serves Sakundeva, whose fundamental greatness she claims to have recognized since her childhood. Sakundeva herself rejects an economy of debt, saying, 'I distrust all those whom I pay and those who serve me' (p. 69). Her relationship with Pandala is thus explicable only in terms of an alternative economy, where debts are not measured, where Pandala's generosity is pure gift: although the sustainability of such an economy is never really explored in the play.

The third character in the play is the Minister, who seeks out Sakundeva in order to persuade her to surrender, and thus to avoid death. His motivations are uncertain, and may be simply a desire for fame, or notoriety. Yet, there is also a suggestion that he has understood the reasons for Sakundeva's necessary alienation. He speaks of the possibility that 'if she survived, one could sow the seeds of a new kind of politics', and shares her lack of abstract respect for the arbitrary mechanisms of the law (p. 81).

The outcome of the Minister's negotiations is never made clear. In return for her surrender, Sakundeva demands financial support for her family, and the establishment of a school for girls in her home town of Madhubai. The Minister seems to assent, but the bargain between the outlaw and the representative of the state remains precarious. Pandala cannot foresee what will happen, and the ending of the play leaves the Minister uncertain as to whether Sakundeva will turn up for her formal surrender:

> Maybe she won't go?
> I see that it's not today I will know.
> I see that it's not in this play that I'll know.
> It's in the next, if I am still minister.
>
> (p. 95)

The story of *La Prise de l'école de Madhubaï* is borrowed from a legendary Indian tale, and is used by Cixous to explore the legitimacy of acting, not just without reference to the Law, but in opposition to it. The play is very tightly focused on the character of Sakundeva, and on the intensity of her relationship with Pandala, and as such seems to vindicate her actions.

121

However, the more general questions of power, legitimacy, and the possibility of sustaining an alternative subjective and social economy, are never fully addressed by the play. Sakundeva's social situation and history are described, rather than dramatized. Her acts of violence are not presented on the stage. The social relations of the rural village and the power structures of the urban ruling class are likewise absent from the stage. The play thus sits in a somewhat unsatisfactory space between history and metaphor, seeming to offer as social critique a text that functions more as allegory.

The importance of this allegorical element is highlighted in the essay that accompanies the published French text of the play, 'Le chemin de légende'. Here Cixous discusses the specificity of theatre in terms of an openness to the Other. From a general interest in the way that actors distance themselves from their own identities, Cixous goes on to examine the ways in which theatre can offer new forms of recognition, and alternative forms of subjectivity. In a discussion that echoes Kleist's analysis of the Marionette Theatre, Cixous sees theatre as a space in which it is possible to regain the state of innocence, in which fixed identities and particular histories are suspended in favour of the compulsion of theatrical space and time. Again, the contrast is with the world of mass culture, which apparently produces individuals who are able only to reproduce cultural norms, and to fear death. Instead, Cixous argues for the importance of a perspective that includes legend, exaltation, delicacy, and poetry. Such a world she refers to as the 'Indies', the space in which we can recover our 'primitive grandeur' (p. 9).

Here, Cixous echoes many of the arguments of nineteenth-century Romanticism, which looked to primitive cultural forms to provide the space for a critique of contemporary culture. The link is made more explicit by Cixous's reference to *Śakuntalā*, the fifth-century Sanskrit play by Kālidasa, on the back cover of the text of *La Prise de l'école de Madhubaï*. In claiming a continuity between her text and Kālidasa's romantic tale of misrecognition, Cixous is placing herself within a tradition of western appropriation of the narratives and metaphors of the East. *Śakuntalā* was one of the earliest Sanskrit dramas to be translated into English, and became an important example for late-eighteenth-century critics of the power of the spontaneous and the primitive as opposed to the assumed inferiority of the culturally sophisticated.

As a comment on the cultural practices and values of the West, such strategies can be powerful and effective. The danger, however, lies in assuming that they have very much to do with the realities of social relations in India, or in Cambodia. Cixous seems aware of the danger. Having talked of the integrity of the space of the 'Indies' in 'Le chemin de légende', she explores the extent to which it too is vulnerable to change, to competing social pressures, and to modernization, in *La Prise de l'école de Madhubaï*:

> O India, your demons are innumerable, they are everywhere,
> in the daily news, the bureaucracy, in my own home.
> But your gods are on the path to extinction, they've become as
> rare as lions. And they don't know how to read.
>
> (*Conquest*, p. 82)

Yet the tension remains: between the careful mobilization of an alternative economy as a critique of the social and sexual relations of the contemporary western world; and a claim that the resulting drama expresses 'the truth' of the 'Indies'. Sometimes productive, and sometimes disabling, this tension will dominate the rest of Cixous's work for the theatre.

Cixous's two most recent plays, *L'Histoire terrible mais inachevée de Norodom Sihanouk roi du Cambodge* [The Terrible but Unfinished Story of Norodom Sihanouk, King of Cambodia], and *L'Indiade ou l'Inde de leurs rêves* [The Indiad, or the India of their Dreams], have both involved the analysis of historical change and political structures, have both been located in distant cultures, and have both been performed by the Théâtre du Soleil. The collaboration between Cixous and the Théâtre du Soleil has been particularly fortunate, since it has provided Cixous with an institutional space for her research into the potential of the theatrical space, and has offered to the Théâtre du Soleil a writer who can respond to the experiments in characterization and staging for which the group is famous.

The Théâtre du Soleil was founded in 1964. At that time, it was one of a number of experimental and political theatre groups in Paris, which were influenced both by the expressive possibilities of total theatre and the formal and political potential of Brechtian epic. The group was formed as a collective, but Ariane Mnouchkine, who directs the group today, was a key member from the start. The group chose their name as a homage to the work of film-makers such as Renoir and Ophuls, whose distinctive use of light seemed to hold out hope for the power of the aesthetic to initiate, to revigorate, and to transform. The fact that Cixous has also demonstrated such a profound interest in the figure of the sun as a force of life and of generation is perhaps a useful indicator of the likely success of their eventual collaboration.

Immediately before the founding of the Théâtre du Soleil, Mnouchkine had been travelling extensively in the East, visiting, among other places, Cambodia. She thus developed an interest in, and an extensive knowledge of, the practices and traditions of eastern theatre, which were used to augment the expressive potential of the group from the beginning. The group's first success was with Wesker's *The Kitchen*, a basically realist text which they approached in a spirit of research and of political commitment. Members of the group visited restaurant kitchens, in order to record the precise gestures and habits of those working there, which were then reproduced on stage in minute detail, though in stylized form. The result of this studied and formalized use of gesture was a combination of social critique and theatrical power reminiscent of Brecht's 'social gest': 'By social gest is meant the mimetic and gestural expression of the social relationship prevailing between people of a given period'.[23]

The events of 1968 provoked the group into more immediate political researches and, after a period of performing agit-prop sketches, they developed a collective exploration of the professional and political role of the actor, which was performed as *Les Clowns*. This was followed by the group's best-known production, *1789*. This play explored new ways of understanding and narrating history, particularly the history of the French Revolution. Instead of a seamless teleological narrative, or a story of great leaders, the Théâtre du Soleil tried to develop techniques for staging 'history from below'. Thus the atmosphere of the performance was carnivalesque. The action took place on a number of small platforms, linked by catwalks, round which the audience could move quite freely. The aim was to involve the audience in the dynamic unfolding of events, to offer them a choice in the way they interpreted or reacted to their own history. Actors played a vast number of parts, and puppets and masks were used to enhance the sense of critical distance between actor and role. Fairground techniques included acrobatics, singing, and a general sense that the actors were offering their wares, their techniques, and their research, for the audience to use as they chose. Of course, this choice was somewhat constrained, since the play was structured round a commitment to the transformative potential of popular action, and was undoubtedly celebratory in its tone. This tone has been criticized as tending to simplify historical process, and to erase the specificity of the actors' social position in favour of an unfocused endorsement of popular revolt.[24] Certainly, the production left some important historical questions unasked, though some of these were addressed by the later production of *1793*. It did, however, manage to find an innovative form for the exploration of historical material, which could engage with the contemporary interests of its audience: a form which was to influence political theatre groups in Europe throughout the 1970s.

The group has always remained committed to a policy of long rehearsal periods, and low ticket prices. The financial implications of this policy became particularly acute in the mid-1970s, and the group survived only by registering its members as unemployed during the lengthy rehearsals for *L'Age d'or*. *L'Age d'or* was eventually performed in 1975, and was an attempt to dramatize the political and economic forces at work in contemporary France. The difficulty of dealing with the immediately contemporary moment was addressed by setting the play in the future, and presenting the present as a kind of legendary or symbolic past. This turn towards the legendary was supported by a stage devoid of scenery. The acting space consisted of four 'craters', under a brass-mirrored ceiling. Masks were once more used, as were the stock characters of *Commedia dell'arte*, and the acting techniques and practices described by Meyerhold as 'biomechanics'. This attempt to combine an exploration of the mechanics of the human body with an account of the mechanics of contemporary society led to a certain degree of uncertainty in the production: the legendary pulling against the political, and the theatrical pulling against the need to explore social complexities. Such uncertainty was much less present in the group's production of

Mephisto, which was derived from a novel by Klaus Mann, and dramatized the transformation of a German cabaret actor into a key figure in the Nazi state. The location for much of the action of this play was the theatre, whose complex social position was signalled by the division of the performing space into two separate areas, one representing cabaret and the popular, the other representing the world of power and of the established theatre.

Throughout the 1970s, then, the Théâtre du Soleil experimented with the expressive and political potential of the theatre. In the early 1980s they moved away from the collectively devised text, towards a sustained engagement with Shakespeare's 'history plays'. The reason they gave for this move was the desire to study 'how to depict the world on a stage'.[25] They used the structure of Shakespeare's plays to provide a framework for an analysis of the relations between individual character and social change, and exploited their formalized and mythic power to augment the resources for historical interpretation developed by the group over the previous fifteen years.

Given Cixous's continuing commitment to the expressive and political potential of Shakespeare's texts, her interest in exploring the capacity of theatre to represent an alternative social and subjective economy, and her fascination with 'the East' as a model of such alternative economies, her collaboration with the Théâtre du Soleil seems to have been heavily overdetermined. It was certainly to produce her most ambitious, and her most successful, theatrical texts.

L'Histoire terrible mais inachevée de Norodom Sihanouk roi du Cambodge was first performed by the Théâtre du Soleil in 1985. It deals with the history of Cambodia, from 1955 to the Vietnamese invasion in 1979. The play is in two parts: the first dealing with the period of Sihanouk's rule of Cambodia, the second dealing with the rule of the Khmers Rouges. The focal point of both parts of the play is, however, Sihanouk, whose struggle to preserve for Cambodia a form of neutrality is set against the self-interested machinations of foreign powers, and the self-righteous illusions of the Khmers Rouges.

The choice of Cambodia as a subject by a writer and a theatre group associated with the Left in France is both interesting and problematic. At one level, it can be seen as an exploration of their own history, since the legacy of French colonial rule is an important determinant in the contemporary history of both Vietnam and Cambodia. Cambodia also carries a huge symbolic weight: its defence against US aggression was an important cause for the Left in the early 1970s, while revelations about the atrocities committed by the Khmers Rouges were to provoke a profound crisis of faith among Left intellectuals later in the decade. The fact that the most influential leaders of the Khmers Rouges had all studied, and learnt their Marxism, in Paris, tended to exacerbate the confused reactions of horror and responsibility.

Dramatizing Cambodia was a project which contained both the strange and the familiar. The legacy of colonialism, with its residual threat of appropriation, meant that the Théâtre du Soleil was keen to represent, and to respect, Cambodia as Other. The perceived culpability of the West in Cambodia's slide into murder and oppression, however, meant that the group was keen to explore the relations between western political and economic structures and the fate of Indochina. The resulting play demonstrates the trace of these competing emphases: moving between using Cambodia as a test case of the deadly effects of imperialist expansionism, and constructing it as the site of an alternative economy of social, and ethical, relations.

Sihanouk is an important figure in the construction of Cambodia as the fragile repository of such an alternative economy. In the play he emerges as a sometimes naïve, and sometimes self-deluding, but basically honest, character. The play opens with a scene in which Sihanouk plays the part of the benevolent monarch with humour, and to apparently good effect. He refers to the Cambodian peasantry as his children, and invites them to bring him their complaints. The way in which he deals with these complaints demonstrates his understanding of the competing forces operating within Cambodia, as he refuses an American sugar company permission to take over agricultural land in order to build a new factory.

Sihanouk is also linked to the forces of generosity, and of tradition, an alliance demonstrated by the frequency and reverence with which he consults the ghost of his dead father. In reality, Sihanouk's father did not die until 1960, but Cixous chooses to make him a ghost from the beginning of the play, in order to stress the peculiarity, and the intensity, of Sihanouk's

127

relation with his family and with his past. This will later be contrasted with the leaders of the Khmers Rouges who reject the relevance of personal ties, and fear to bring children into the world they are creating. Cixous adds more and more ghosts to her cast of characters until, by the end of the play, they outnumber the living on stage, an indication of the fact that 'les vivants chaque jour sont plus proches des morts' [the living each day are closer to the dead] (p. 333).

Sihanouk is accompanied at various points throughout the play by a musician, who functions both as chorus and as Shakespearian fool. The musician likens the Prince himself to a fool, and Sihanouk is certainly guilty of blindness and self-deception on a scale worthy of King Lear. At other times, however, he is capable of significant, and even poetic insight: when he describes Cambodia as 'this other Eden, demi-paradise' its disastrous fate is assured (p. 65). These same terms are used by John of Gaunt in Shakespeare's *Richard II* to describe the happy state of England, but he goes on to predict its ruin under Richard's reign. Sihanouk also talks of his fondness for music, for literature, for the stars, while Pol Pot talks only of discipline and hatred.

The extreme nature of the contrast between these two characters, and the values they represent, is theatrically very effective. Since the play was performed on a stage surrounded by figurative representations of the Cambodian dead, the sense of the enormity of the stakes involved helped to validate such extremes as Pol Pot's panegyric to hatred in Act 1, sc. ii. As historical analysis, however, such polarization is less helpful. There is a tendency to equate harmful political ideas with unpleasant or easily manipulated people, which does little to explain the success of the Khmers Rouges's ideological and political project of gaining peasant support. This problem is particularly acute in the representation of the American characters who are either ineffective liberals, or power-mad and violent conservatives.

Although Sihanouk carries much of the force of the alternative social and subjective relations associated with Cambodia, there are other characters who contribute to the charm and the otherness of the Cambodia represented in the play. There are two pairs of women who are important throughout the play. Sihanouk's mother is linked with a character called Mom

Savay, who had been her husband's lover, but is now her closest friend. They meet up, perhaps a little implausibly, with a couple of working-class women, one of whom is the mother of a leader of the Khmers Rouges, and the other of whom is a Vietnamese woman living and working in Cambodia. These four women become emblematic of the possibility of a social order that would respect difference, without referring it to a hierarchical structure. Religious difference, national difference, and class difference are all acknowledged, but the relationship between the women survives despite such differences, and manages even to erase the ultimate difference between the living and the dead.

Although Cixous's response to characters like Pol Pot is not in any doubt, there are certain explicit links between the overall project of the Khmers Rouges and some of Cixous's own earlier texts which complicate her analysis of the legitimacy and the implications of revolutionary change in very interesting ways. In Act 2, sc. ii, of Part One, Sihanouk talks of the necessity to defend the neutrality of Cambodia against the actions of moles: the figure of the mole was the one Cixous had earlier chosen to represent her own subversive activity. In Act 2, sc. v, of Part Two, Pol Pot speaks of the need to purge the egotistical desire for property, a demand that echoes Cixous's own critique of 'le propre'. Such parallels suggest that, for Cixous, the encounter with the history of Cambodia is a very personal encounter with the legitimacy of revolutionary struggle. The play offers no definitive answers to this dilemma: it suggests how badly things can go wrong, but it does not condemn the desire for change. In the end, however, it pins its hope on the possibility of survival. Sihanouk bemoans a paradise lost, but we are told that the story is not finished: as long as the Cambodian language and culture survive, there is still hope.

Cixous's shift in this play from sexual politics to national struggle has disconcerted many of her readers. With hindsight, however, it seems like an uncannily prophetic move: a recognition of the ways in which ethnicity and national struggle were to unsettle the categories of Left and feminist thought in the late 1980s. The move is certainly reinforced by the subject matter of Cixous's next play, *L'Indiade*. In her critical and theoretical writings, this change of emphasis is signalled by her increasing interest in the concept of resistance, and in the need to preserve and to protect vulnerable peoples and cultures against the forces of homogenization and oppression. This interest is partly strategic and metaphorical, with her analysis of other cultures becoming a way of intervening in contemporary French culture and politics, but it is also profoundly serious. She sees the possibility of an alliance between different forms of otherness, which would protect and respect difference, but would be strong enough to represent significant resistance.

Cixous has linked her interest in Cambodia to a more general project of protecting that which is threatened with effacement, and of restoring historical memory.[26] In fact, the reality of Cambodia's vulnerability to effacement has been challenged by Anthony Barnett. Barnett has argued that the idea of Cambodia's fragility and imminent disappearance is the product of mythical origins wished on the Cambodian people by a French colonial power, which aimed to offer its own support as a remedy for Cambodia's historical decline.[27] His argument is not that Cambodia does not face a serious threat to its autonomy and integrity, but that the mobilization of the trope of 'imminent disappearance' does not advance the understanding of the contemporary moment of Cambodian history.

But Cixous's interest in writing as the site of preservation goes beyond her interest in Cambodia. It refers more generally to her convictions about the specificity of theatre. She describes theatre as the space not of sexuality but of the heart, by which she means that it can find forms to move beyond the exploration of subjectivity towards the exploration of the intersubjective structures of ethical and political relations.[28] Such explorations are aided by the alienation of the ego required of the actor when performing on stage. Cixous relates this process of distancing from the stable and fixed ego to the economy of femininity, when she says that every actor is part saint and part woman ('L'incarnation', p. 265). Finally, Cixous defines the political and ethical role of the theatre in terms of this capacity for openness to the Other, and insists, in a manner reminiscent of T. S. Eliot, that the power of a theatrical text is a function of the impersonality with which it renders other people's histories and cultures:

Humble scribe d'une douleur mondiale que je suis, je ne dois pas avoir de cœur, seulement des oreilles pour recueillir les plaintes des désespérés, et pour les transcrire.[29]

[Humble scribe of a grief of global proportions as I am, I should not have a heart, but only ears to gather up the complaints of those without hope, and to transcribe them.]

The possibility of sustaining otherness is very much at stake in Cixous's most recent play, *L'Indiade*, which was also written in conjunction with the Théâtre du Soleil. First performed in 1987, this play dramatizes the history of India from 1937 to 1948, a period which saw the culmination of the Indian struggle for independence from British rule, the partition of India into India and Pakistan, and the assassination of Gandhi.

Once more, this play has elements both of historiography and mythography.[30] In historical terms, the play explores the political and ideological structures which underlay the drive towards the partition of India, and the legacy of violence which these structures produced. Thus it dramatizes the different conceptions of national identity which lay behind the policies of Gandhi, of Nehru, and of the Muslim League. Jinnah, the spokesman of the Muslim League, is represented as driven by fear: he fears powerlessness, he fears assimilation, he dreams of death and violence. His sense of Muslim identity is based on separation and exclusion. His drive towards the establishment of a separate Muslim nation is seen in the play as regressive, as necessarily violent, but it is also seen as following a certain, and perhaps even dominant, logic. Jinnah's sense of political identity is premissed on the obliteration of the Other, and he doesn't want to be obliterated.

Jinnah's political interests are made clear at the start of the play, and the drama lies in the attempts of Gandhi and Nehru to impose a different conception of nationhood. Gandhi's thinking is organicist:

Le mystère. L'autre sexe, l'autre religion, l'autre être humain. Il y a un arbre, deux feuilles ne sont pas identiques mais elles dansent sur la même brise: c'est l'arbre humain. Donnons le temps aux choses humaines de germer, de mûrir. (p. 82)

[The mystery. The other sex, the other religion, the other human being. There is a tree, two leaves are not identical, but they dance in the same breeze: it is the tree of humanity. Let's give human things the time to germinate, to ripen.]

Throughout the play he struggles to assert a version of Indian political and national identity which will sustain a central root, while allowing different branches to grow as they wish. The dilemma has much in common with Cixous's own attempts to find ways of theorizing femininity which will allow common political and cultural struggle, without constraining plurality and difference. Gandhi is clear that the task is huge: 'il faut changer de cœur' [we must alter our hearts] (p. 43), and it is indeed one in which he is to fail. This failure is recognized by Nehru, and attributed to the human weakness – insufficient love (p. 164).

The progress of this historical struggle involves a series of characters who embody different facets of Indian religious, political, gender, and class identity. Thus, the woman poet Sarojini Naïdu is present throughout, and represents the voice of the educated middle classes who supported Nehru. The strength of her commitment is signalled by her decision to give up writing for twenty years to dedicate her energies to the struggle for independence; the enormity of this investment is signalled by her recognition that it is too late for her to write again. The interests of the illiterate and uneducated are articulated by the Bengali woman character, Haridasi. She acts as a prophetic chorus, commenting on the decisions taken, mocking the *naïveté* and self-deception of those who take them. She constantly pleads for the illiterate, and for the women who seem absent in so many of the discussions in the play. Although Haridasi has an identifiable social and regional position, she does also function as a sort of 'everywoman': her opening speech identifies her village as the whole of India, and her search for the mythical origins of India, 'quand il n'y avait ni Anglais ni hindou ni musulman ni masculin ni féminin' [when there were neither English nor Hindu nor Muslim nor masculine nor feminine] (p. 19), suggests that she is placed outside the history and the knowledges that determine the action of the play.

The mythographic element in *L'Indiade* is, perhaps, already clear. The partition of India becomes a metaphor for the competition between different economies of subjective and social relations, economies which Cixous has elsewhere classified as 'masculine' and 'feminine'. Gandhi undoubtedly emerges as the hero in this struggle. Like the actor, Gandhi has within him elements of the maternal. In a gesture reminiscent of the mother brought before Solomon, he chooses to give up his child, India, rather than to see it torn apart (p. 160).

The vulnerability of such an alternative economy is, however, represented by the figure of a female bear, who enters the play in Act 2. Cixous has written about the bear as a symbol of self, of other, of innocence, and of cruelty, and has speculated on the reasons for its charm and theatrical power.[31] At first, the bear seems like a benign presence. The Théâtre du Soleil staged the bear with great care, using actors who could exploit the tension between the audience's desire to believe in its reality and their fascination with the skilled performance which could ape animal movement while retaining the vestiges of human identity. As the play progresses, however, the bear becomes increasingly unsettled. Eventually, she is driven mad by the fear and violence that surround her, and, having killed two men, she turns on her own handler, who has to kill her. The story of the bear immediately brings to mind Kleist's thoughts on the limitations of human consciousness, where he attributes more grace to a puppet, or to a bear, than to any human burdened with the legacy of self-consciousness. This connection is strengthened by the handler's insistence that although the bear had to be killed she was never really anything other than innocent, which sets in play the series of questions raised by Kleist about innocence, knowledge, and grace (p. 191). Thus, as well as figuring the legacy of violence brought about by an economy of exclusion and separation, the bear becomes a figure of 'paradise lost', of the fall from grace represented by human consciousness. She also functions as a figure of the unconscious, in her relation to her handler. She is that part of himself which is kept chained up, which is creative, and powerful, but ultimately dangerous. Finally, the figure of the bear, particularly when set beside imagery of the stars, seems to echo Flaubert's exploration of the inadequacies of human speech in *Madame Bovary*:

la parole humaine est comme un chaudron fêlé où nous battons des mélodies à faire danser les ours, quand on voudrait attendrir les étoiles.

[human speech is like a cracked kettle on which we beat out tunes for bears to dance to, when all the time we are longing to move the stars to pity.][32]

Such density of symbolism contributes much to the fascination of this text, but little to its clarity. When we turn to the further levels of symbolism implicit in the very choice of India as a subject, and those specifically exploited in the overall structure and performance of the play, the situation becomes yet more complex. *L'Indiade* dramatizes a struggle between two different subjective and political economies. In its overall setting, however, it seems to embody, to give shape to, one of these economies. Cixous has written of the different dimensions and structures of Indian ethical and religious thought in terms of a different relation to the stars, an aspiration towards values that exceed the narrowly human, and these are the dimensions she tries to articulate in *L'Indiade*.

Images of the heavens and the stars are used frequently by Cixous. In a discussion of *Romeo and Juliet*, the stars are used as a metaphor for the complexities of time, the visual presence of stars in the present representing the tangible legacy of events light years in the past.[33] In *L'Indiade*, however, 'the stars' are a figure of the dimensions of thought that escape the instrumentalist rationality that Cixous sees as dominant in European culture. For cultural and historical reasons, she argues, Indian people have a sense of the stars: their thought encompasses the enigmatic and the unknown. These are the dimensions of Indian identity that the Théâtre du Soleil sought to capture in their staging of the play.

The performing area for *L'Indiade* was a huge empty white stage, at the bottom of steeply raked seats which accommodated the audience. The Cartoucherie had been completely transformed in keeping with the Indian setting: Indian food was sold in the foyer by actors in costume; traditional Indian friezes decorated the walls; a massive map of India was displayed inside the entrance. The foyer exuded bustle, while the performing area communicated a sense of vastness. Throughout the performance props and scenery were minimal. Meetings were signalled by the rolling-on of carpets and cushions, street life by the strenuous and acrobatic movements of actors pulling rickshaws. The virtuosity of the physical presence of the actors competed constantly with the minimalism of the staging to create a sense of impending violence and unexpressed energies. Much of the action was accompanied by music, played on a vast range of Indian instruments, which was clearly intended to provide a sense of authenticity, as well as contributing to the coherence of the performance as a whole.

The staging of *L'Indiade* thus tended to emphasize the sense of India as an intact, and foreign, space. Great care was taken in the representation of the minute details of gesture and social behaviour, and in the rhythms of speech. Each aspect of the performance offered a sense of both recognition and strangeness: a dual response characteristic not just of the uncanny, but also of the cultural legacies of colonialism.

Such attention to the detail of movement and gesture, coupled with the constant move towards metaphorization, reproduced at the level of performance the tension inherent in the structure of this play. The full title of the play is *L'Indiade ou l'Inde de leurs rêves*, which already complicates the ontological status of the space of the play. The claim that the dreams explored in this play are those of the Indian people, however, still seems open to question. Perhaps this text can be better understood and appreciated as a text about *our* dreams: the versions of otherness we need in order to sustain political and cultural struggle, and the possibility of an identity based on the recognition of difference.

Writing for the theatre, then, has both extended and transformed Cixous's writing project. It has allowed her to explore different relations to otherness, to develop her theorization of the bodily dimensions of language, to posit the existence of alternative social and subjective economies, and to tie her theoretical work to the mechanisms of historical change. These developments have led Cixous's work away from the intense focus on feminine subjectivity and its relations to the female body that were so important to her work in the 1970s. Instead, she is now committed to understanding women's struggle as part of a broader political and ethical movement: to realize the subjective and collective dimensions of a feminine economy, to preserve cultural diversity in the face of homogenization, and to resist the deadly cynicism of subjective and social domination.

Scenes from *L'Indiade*, performed by the Théâtre du Soleil at the Cartoucherie, Paris, in 1987 (Reproduced by courtesy of Magnum)

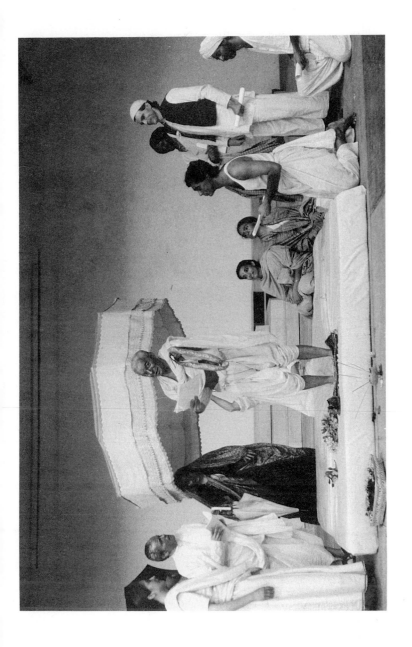

NOTES

INTRODUCTION

1 A very helpful discussion of the range of Cixous's fictional writing, and many of its intertextual resonances, can be found in Claudine Guégan Fisher, *La Cosmogonie d'Hélène Cixous* (Amsterdam: Rodopi, 1988).

1 POLITICS AND WRITING

1 For an interesting discussion of the aspects of Cixous's work known in Britain and the USA, see Nicole Ward Jouve, 'Hélène Cixous: from inner theatre to world theatre', in *White Woman Speaks with Forked Tongue: Criticism as Autobiography* (London: Routledge, 1990), pp. 91–100.

2 'Sorties', in C. Clément and H. Cixous, *La Jeune Née* (Paris: Union Générale d'Editions, 10/18, 1975), pp. 115–246; translated by Betsy Wing in *The Newly Born Woman* (Manchester: Manchester University Press, 1986), pp. 63–132.

3 For Derrida's reading of Hegel, to which Cixous's account is closely related, see *Glas,* trans. J. P. Leavey and R. Rand (London: University of Nebraska Press, 1986).

4 See 'Le sexe ou la tête?', *Les Cahiers du GRIF*, no. 13 (1976), 5–15; translated by Annette Kuhn as 'Castration or Decapitation?', *Signs: Journal of Women in Culture and Society*, vol. 7 (1981), 41–55.

5 For a consideration of the philosophical and political importance of metaphorical thinking in Cixous's work, see Françoise Defromont, 'Metaphorical Thinking and Poetic Writing in Virginia Woolf and Hélène Cixous', in Helen Wilcox *et al.* (eds), *The Body and the Text: Hélène Cixous, Reading and Teaching* (London: Harvester Wheatsheaf, 1990), pp. 114–125.

6 Sigmund Freud, 'Female Sexuality', *The Standard Edition of the Complete Psychological Works of Sigmund Freud*, ed. J. Strachey [=SE], vol. 21 (London: Hogarth, 1955), pp. 221–243 (p. 226).

7 See *The Penguin Complete Stories of Franz Kafka*, ed. N. N. Glatzer

(London: Allen Lane, 1983), pp. 3–4. For another reading of this text, see, J. Derrida, 'Devant la loi', in A. Phillips Griffiths (ed.), *Philosophy and Literature*, Royal Institute of Philosophy Lecture Series 16 (Cambridge: Cambridge University Press, 1984), pp. 173–88.

8 See Aeschylus, *The Oresteia*, trans. R. Fagles (Harmondsworth: Penguin, 1977), particularly the second play of the trilogy, *Choephori* [The Libation Bearers]; and Sophocles, *Electra*, in *Greek Tragedies: Volume Two*, ed. D. Grene and R. Lattimore (London: University of Chicago Press, 1960), pp. 45–109.

9 Sigmund Freud, 'Moses and Monotheism', *SE*, vol. 23, pp. 7–137 (pp. 113–14).

10 J.-J. Bachofen, *Das Mutterrecht* [Mother Right] (Stuttgart, 1861); and F. Engels, *The Origin of the Family, Private Property and the State* (Harmondsworth: Penguin, 1985).

11 The same conclusion is arrived at, for rather different reasons, by Simon Goldhill in *Language, Sexuality, Narrative: The 'Oresteia'* (Cambridge: Cambridge University Press, 1984).

12 See 'Le rire de la Méduse', *L'Arc*, 61 (1975), 39–54; translated as 'The Laugh of the Medusa,' in E. Marks and I. de Courtivron (eds), *New French Feminisms* (Brighton: Harvester, 1980), pp. 245–64 (p. 245).

13 Heinrich Von Kleist, 'Penthesilea', in *Plays*, ed. W. Hinderer (New York: Continuum, 1982), pp. 165–268.

14 See, for example, Toril Moi, *Sexual/Textual Politics: Feminist Literary Theory* (London: Methuen, 1985).

15 Barbara Freeman, 'Plus corps donc plus écriture: Hélène Cixous and the Mind–Body problem', *Paragraph*, vol. 11, no. 1 (1988), 58–70 (p. 62).

16 Roland Barthes, *Roland Barthes*, trans. R. Howard (London: Macmillan, 1977). This quotation, to be found near the end of the book, is placed opposite an illustration from Diderot's *Encyclopédie*, entitled 'Anatomy.'

17 Jane Gallop, '"Writing and Sexual Difference": The Difference Within', in E. Abel (ed.), *Writing and Sexual Difference* (Brighton: Harvester, 1982), pp. 283–90 (p. 288).

18 Domna C. Stanton, 'Difference on Trial: A Critique of the Maternal Metaphor in Cixous, Irigaray and Kristeva', in N. K. Miller (ed.), *The Poetics of Gender* (New York: Columbia University Press, 1986), pp. 157–82. This should be read alongside her earlier article, 'Language and Revolution: The Franco-American Dis-Connection', in H. Eisenstein and A. A. Jardine (eds), *The Future of Difference* (New York: Barnard College Women's Center, 1980), pp. 73–87, which advances a very different argument.

19 Alice A. Jardine, *Gynesis: Configurations of Woman and Modernity* (London: Cornell University Press, 1985).

20 Claudine Guégan Fisher, *La Cosmogonie d'Hélène Cixous* (Amsterdam: Rodopi, 1988), and Verena Andermatt Conley, *Hélène Cixous: Writing the Feminine* (Lincoln, Nebraska: University of Nebraska

Press, 1984). These are the only other book-length studies of Cixous's work. Fisher is very thorough and very enlightening in her readings of Cixous's fiction; Conley provides a useful and extended account of the philosophical context of Cixous's work.

21 Marcel Mauss, *The Gift: The Form and Reason for Exchange in Archaic Societies*, trans. W. D. Halls (London: Routledge, 1990); Georges Bataille, *The Accursed Share: An Essay on General Economy*, trans. R. Hurley, 3 vols, vol. 1 (New York: Zone Books, 1988), pp. 63–77; Derrida, *Glas*, trans. J.P. Leavey and R. Rand (London: University of Nebraska Press, 1986) especially pp. 242–4. See also M. Richman, 'Sex and Signs: The Language of French Feminist Criticism', *Language and Style*, vol. 13, no. 4 (1980), 62–80; and Judith Still, 'A Feminine Economy: Some Preliminary Thoughts', in Helen Wilcox *et al.* (eds), *The Body and the Text*, pp. 49–60.

22 'La Venue à l'écriture', in Hélène Cixous, Madeleine Gagnon and Annie Leclerc, *La Venue à l'écriture* (Paris: Union Générale d'Editions, 10/18, 1977); Cixous's article has been reprinted in *Entre l'écriture* (Paris: des femmes, 1986), pp. 9–69.

23 Hélène Cixous, 'Difficult Joys', in Helen Wilcox *et al.* (eds), *The Body and the Text*, pp. 5–30 (p. 12).

24 *Le Troisième Corps* is also the title of a novel by Cixous, published in 1970.

25 See 'des femmes en mutation', *Livres: Hebdo*, 22 Feb. 1988, p. 69.

26 Antoinette Fouque used this phrase in an interview with Catherine Clément, published in *Le Matin*, 16 July 1980, p. 13. A translation can be found in C. Duchen (ed.), *French Connections: Voices from the Women's Movement in France* (London: Hutchinson, 1987), pp. 50–4. For further analysis of the role of *Psyche et Po* at this time see Nicole Ward Jouve, 'Psych et Po and French Feminisms', in *White Woman Speaks with Forked Tongue*, pp. 61–74.

27 See Françoise van Rossum Guyon, 'Entretien avec Hélène Cixous', *Revue des Sciences Humaines*, no. 168 (1977), 479–93. Unusually, Cixous comes across as dogmatic in this interview, and the impression of remorselessly sticking to an agreed position is strong.

28 H. Eisenstein and A. A. Jardine (eds), *The Future of Difference* (New York: Barnard College Women's Center, 1980).

29 Useful documents relating to these conflicts within the women's movement in France can be found in C. Duchen (ed.), *French Connections*. Relevant journals, pamphlets, and books can be found in the Bibliothèque Marguerite Durand, Paris.

30 For Cixous's own account of Vincennes see 'Vincennes, héritière de 68, dans le vertige de la scène avec le père', *des femmes en mouvements*, no. 11 (1978), 70–3.

31 For details, see *Le Matin*, 25 July 1980.

32 'Tancrède continue', *Etudes Freudiennes*, nos 21–2 (1983), 115–31; reprinted in *Entre l'écriture*, pp. 139–68; translated as 'Tancredi Continues', in Susan Sellers (ed.), *Writing Differences: Readings from the Seminar of Hélène Cixous* (Milton Keynes: Open University Press,

1988), pp. 37–53. See also '12 Août 1980', bilingual text, trans. B. Wing, *Boundary 2*, vol 12, no. 2 (1984). 8–39. For a discussion of this text see K. J. Crecelius, 'La voix de Tancrède: de Cixous à Sand', in F. van Rossum-Guyon and M. Diaz-Diocaretz (eds), *Hélène Cixous: chemins d'une écriture* (Amsterdam: Rodopi, 1990), pp. 75–82.

33 Torquato Tasso, *Jerusalem Delivered*, trans. E. Fairfax (London: Centaur, 1962), particularly Books I–III and Book XII. A recording of Rossini's *Tancredi*, with Marilyn Horne singing the title role, is available from CBS Records.

34 Both the *Oxford Dictionary of Music* (Oxford: Oxford University Press, 1985) and the *New Penguin Dictionary of Music* (Harmondsworth: Penguin, 1978) claim that Rossini derives his opera from Tasso.

35 C. B. Beall, *La Fortune du Tasse en France*, Studies in Literature and Philology no. 4 (Eugene, Oregon: University of Oregon, 1942), p. 158.

36 It is perhaps interesting to note the reference to *Tancredi* in Balzac's *Sarrasine*, a text whose relations to the representation of sexual difference have been explored by Roland Barthes: see *S/Z* (Paris: Editions du Seuil, 1970), p. 233.

37 'Le dernier tableau ou le portrait de Dieu', in *Entre l'écriture* (Paris: des femmes, 1986) pp. 169–201

38 Martin Heidegger, *Poetry, Language, Thought*, trans. A. Hofstadter (New York: Harper & Row, 1971), p. 36.

39 See, for example, Samuel Beckett, *Proust* (London: Dolphin, 1931).

2 STRATEGIES OF READING

1 *L'Exil de James Joyce ou l'art du remplacement* (Paris: Bernard Grasset, 1968), trans. Sally Purcell as *The Exile of James Joyce* (London: John Calder, 1976); *Prénoms de Personne* (Paris: Editions du Seuil, 1974); *Entre l'écriture* (Paris: des femmes, 1986).

2 The texts in this volume dealing with Joyce are, 'Texte du hors', pp. 233–6; 'Les hérésistances du sujet', pp. 237–86; 'La crucifiction', pp. 287–311; and 'Trait portrait de l'artiste en son autre j'aimot', pp. 313–31. An extended version of 'La crucifiction' forms the introduction to *Dublinois: Les Morts, Contreparties/Dubliners: The Dead, Counterparts* (Paris: Aubier-Flammarion, 1974). This introduction is one of the most suggestive and exciting of Cixous's readings of Joyce. 'Les hérésistances du sujet' has been partly translated: pp. 274–86 have been translated by Carol Bové as 'At Circe's or the Self-Opener', *Boundary 2*, vol. 3 (1975), 387–97; an earlier version (published in *Poétique* in 1970) of pp. 238–54 has been translated by Judith Still as 'Joyce: the (R)use of Writing', in D. Attridge and D. Ferrer (eds), *Post-Structuralist Joyce: Essays from the French* (Cambridge: Cambridge University Press, 1984), pp. 15–29.

3 The texts dealing with Joyce are 'La missexualité: où jouis-je?', pp. 75–95; and 'Freincipe de plaisir ou paradoxe perdu', pp. 99–112.

4 In the light of Joyce's earlier publication of *A Portrait of the Artist as a Young Man*, it is interesting that Shaun's attempt at control should include the attempt to fit M. into a portrait. The implications of portraiture will continue to preoccupy Cixous, from her reading of Henry James's 'Preface' to *Portrait of a Lady*, 'Henry James: l'écriture comme placement', *Poétique*, 1 (1970), 35–50, to her writing of *Portrait de Dora*.

5 'The Uncanny' in *The Standard Edition of the Complete Psychological Works of Sigmund Freud*, ed. J. Strachey [=SE], vol. 17, (London: Hogarth, 1955), pp. 217–52.

6 E. Jentsch, 'Zur Psychologie des unheimlichen', *Psychiatrisch-neurologische Wochenschrift*, 8, 195 (1906), 219–21, 226–7.

7 'La fiction et ses fantômes', *Prénoms de personne*, pp. 13–38; translated by R. Dennomé as 'Fiction and its Phantoms: A Reading of Freud's *Das Unheimlich* (The "Uncanny")', *New Literary History*, vol. 7 (1976), 528–48; 'Les noms du pire', *Prénoms*, pp. 29–99; 'L'incertitude intellectuelle', *Prénoms*, pp. 100–11; part of this essay, together with part of the succeeding essay, 'Les comptes d'Hoffmann' (pp. 112–26) are translated by K. Cohen as 'The Character of "Character"', *New Literary History*, vol. 5 (1974) 383–402. For details of the Hoffmann texts, see *Tales of Hoffmann*, trans. R. J. Hollingdale (Harmondsworth: Penguin, 1982), and 'Kreisleriana', in *Fantaisies dans la manière de Callot*, trans. H. de Curzon (Paris: Phébus, 1979), pp. 47–97 and 361–412.

8 J. Derrida, 'The Double Session', trans. B. Johnson (London: Athlone, 1981), pp. 173–285. See also Cixous's discussion of Hoffmann's 'Kreisleriana' in 'Les comptes d'Hoffmann'.

9 Heinrich Von Kleist, 'About the Marionette Theatre', *Life and Letters Today*, vol. 16 (1937), 101–5; Hélène Cixous, 'Les marionnettes', *Prénoms*, pp. 127–52.

10 Edgar Allan Poe, 'The Murders in the Rue Morgue', *Tales of Mystery and Imagination* (London: Dent, 1963), pp. 378–410 (pp. 378–81).

11 See Edgar Allan Poe, *Oeuvres en prose*, trans. C. Baudelaire, ed. Y.-G. Le Dantec (Paris: Gallimard, Pléiade, 1956), pp. 1105–6.

12 See R. Foye (ed.), *The Unknown Poe* (San Francisco: City Lights, 1980), pp. 79–92.

13 For discussion of this concept see Walter Benjamin, *Charles Baudelaire: A Lyric Poet in the Era of High Capitalism*, trans. H. Zohn (London: NLB, 1973).

14 See Alexis de Tocqueville, *On Democracy, Revolution and Society*, ed. J. Stone and S. Mennell (London: University of Chicago Press, 1980).

15 See Andreas Huyssen, *After the Great Divide: Modernism, Mass Culture, Postmodernism* (Bloomington: Indiana University Press, 1986).

16 J. Lacan, 'Le séminaire sur "La lettre volée"', in *Ecrits* (Paris: Editions du Seuil, 1966), pp. 11–61. This text, and Derrida's reply,

are translated in J. P. Muller and W. J. Richardson (eds), *The Purloined Poe: Lacan, Derrida and Psychoanalytic Reading* (London: Johns Hopkins University Press, 1988).

17 S. Freud, 'Beyond the Pleasure Principle', *SE*, vol. 18, pp. 7–64.

18 The problematic of repetition had also preoccupied both Kierkegaard and Nietzsche: see Søren Kierkegaard, 'Repetition: An Essay in Experimental Psychology' (1843), in *A Kierkegaard Anthology*, ed. R. Bretall (Princeton: Princeton University Press, 1946), pp. 134–52; and Friedrich Nietzsche, 'Eternal Recurrence', in *A Nietzsche Reader*, ed. R. J. Hollingdale (Harmondsworth: Penguin, 1977), pp. 249–62.

19 J. Derrida, 'The Purveyor of Truth', *Yale French Studies*, 52 (1975), 31–113, p. 45.

20 Barbara Johnson, 'The Frame of Reference: Poe, Lacan, Derrida', in *The Critical Difference* (London: Johns Hopkins University Press, 1980), pp. 110–46; Marian Hobson, 'Deconstruction, Empiricism, and the Postal Services', *French Studies*, vol. 36 (1982), 290–314; J. Gallop, 'The American Other', in *Reading Lacan* (London: Cornell University Press, 1985), pp. 55–73.

21 'Paradoxe du jamais plus', *Prénoms*, pp. 183–214 (p. 185). For discussion of Poe, see also 'Une poétique du revenir', *Prénoms*, pp. 155–182 and 'L'Autre analyste', Prénoms, pp. 215–29. 'Ligeia', *Tales of Mystery and Imagination*, pp. 155–69; 'Berenice', pp. 175–82; 'Morella', pp. 182–7.

22 'L'approche de Clarice Lispector', *Poétique*, 40 (1979), 408–19, reprinted in *Entre l'écriture* (Paris: des femmes, 1986), pp. 113–38; and *Vivre l'orange/To Live the Orange*, bilingual text (Paris: des femmes, 1979), reprinted in *L'Heure de Clarice Lispector* (Paris: des femmes, 1989), pp. 7–113.

23 'Extreme Fidelity', in Susan Sellers (ed.), *Writing Differences* (Milton Keynes: Open University Press, 1988), pp. 9–36 (an expanded version of this text has been published as 'L'Auteur en vérité' in *L'Heure de Clarice Lispector*, pp. 122–68); 'Reaching the Point of Wheat, or A Portrait of the Artist as a Maturing Woman', *New Literary History*, vol. 19 (1987), 1–21; 'A la lumière d'une pomme', in *L'Heure de Clarice Lispector*, pp. 115–20. See also *Reading With Clarice Lispector* (London: Harvester Wheatsheaf, 1990): this selection of texts given by Cixous at her seminar is preceded by a helpful introduction by Verena Andermatt Conley.

24 This invocation of Heidegger is necessarily complicated for the contemporary reader by the series of battles that have raged in France over the significance of Heidegger's support for the policies and politics of Fascism. The extent to which this support disables Heidegger's philosophical texts is still a matter of fierce debate. See, for example, Victor Farias, *Heidegger et le nazisme* (Paris: Verdier, 1987); Pierre Bourdieu, *L'Ontologie politique de Martin Heidegger* (Paris: Minuit, 1975, reprinted 1988); Jean-François Lyotard, *Heidegger et 'les juifs'* (Paris: Galilée, 1988); and Philippe Lacoue-Labarthe,

Heidegger, Art and Politics: The Fiction of the Political, trans. C. Turner (Oxford: Basil Blackwell, 1990).

25 Martin Heidegger, *Being and Time*, trans. J. Macquarrie and E. Robinson (Oxford: Basil Blackwell, 1978), p. 31.

26 See 'Reaching the Point of Wheat', pp. 14–20.

27 For an example of the ways in which Lispector represents the disruptive power of encountering objects in their materiality, without the relations of expectation and duty that usually surround them, see 'The Sharing of Bread', in C. Lispector, *The Foreign Legion: Stories and Chronicles*, trans. G Pontiero, (Manchester: Carcanet, 1986), pp. 28–30.

28 See also the discussion in 'Poésie e(s)t politique?', *des femmes en mouvements: hebdo*, no. 4, Nov./Dec. 1979, 29–32.

29 C. Lispector, *The Hour of the Star*, trans. G. Pontiero (Manchester: Carcanet, 1986).

30 *Hour*, p. 84. This phrase is one of the many titles proposed by the author on the title page of this novel. The proposed titles include 'The Blame is Mine'; 'The Right to Protest'; 'A Tearful Tale'; and 'Clarice Lispector'. The generic and subjective complexity of the text is thus foregrounded from the start.

31 For elaboration of this concept, see Edward Said, *Orientalism* (London: Routledge & Kegan Paul, 1978).

32 'C'est là que je vais', in *Où étais-tu pendant la nuit?* (Paris: des femmes, 1985), p. 111.

33 See Clarice Lispector, *Near to the Wild Heart*, trans. G. Pontiero (Manchester: Carcanet, 1990), and James Joyce, *A Portrait of the Artist as a Young Man* (Harmondsworth: Penguin, 1970), p. 171.

3 WRITING DIFFERENTLY

1 This novel has been translated by Carol Barko as *Inside* (New York: Schocken, 1986).

2 Nicole Ward Jouve, 'Hélène Cixous: from inner theatre to world theatre', in *White Woman Speaks with Forked Tongue: Criticism as Autobiography* (London: Routledge, 1990), pp. 91–100 (p. 94).

3 Gilles Deleuze, 'Hélène Cixous ou l'écriture stroboscopique', *Le Monde*, 11 Aug. 1972, p. 10. For discussion of *Neutre*, see Lucette Finas, 'Le pourpre du neutre', in *Le Bruit d'Iris* (Paris: Flammarion, 1978), 303–23.

4 For a fascinating analysis of the theoretical implications of the language and the imagery of this text see Mairéad Hanrahan, 'Une porte du "Portrait du soleil" ou la succulence du sujet', in F. van Rossum-Guyon and M. Diaz-Diocaretz (eds), *Hélène Cixous: chemins d'une écriture* (Amsterdam: Rodopi, 1990), pp. 45–53.

5 Friedrich Nietzsche, *Thus Spoke Zarathustra*, trans. R. J. Hollingdale (Harmondsworth: Penguin, 1969), p. 62.

6 Friedrich Nietzsche, *The Birth of Tragedy and The Case of Wagner*, trans. W. Kaufmann (New York: Vintage Books, 1967), pp. 59–60.

7 Georges Bataille, *The Accursed Share: An Essay on General Economy*, trans. R. Hurley, 3 vols, vol. 1 (New York: Zone Books, 1988), p. 11.

8 See C. Andrews (ed.), *The Ancient Egyptian Book of the Dead*, trans. R. O. Faulkner (London: British Museum, 1985).

9 Martin Bernal, *Black Athena: The Afroasiatic Roots of Classical Civilization*, vol. 1 (London: Free Association Books, 1987).

10 H.D., *Helen in Egypt* (Manchester: Carcanet, 1985).

11 For discussion of this issue, and of the different writing styles set in play by this novel, see Christiane Makward, 'Structures du silence/du délire', *Poétique*, 35 (1978), 314–24.

12 Jacques Lacan, 'Dieu et la jouissance de Lá femme', *Le Séminaire: Livre XX, Encore*, ed. J.-A. Miller (Paris: Editions du Seuil, 1975), pp. 61–71 (p. 68); trans. J. Rose, in J. Mitchell and J. Rose, (eds), *Jacques Lacan and the 'école freudienne'* (London: Macmillan, 1982), pp. 137–48 (p. 144).

13 See Verena Andermatt Conley, *Hélène Cixous: Writing the Feminine* (Lincoln, Nebraska: University of Nebraska Press, 1984), pp. 88–93; and J. Derrida, *Glas*, trans. J. P. Leavey and R. Rand (London: University of Nebraska Press, 1986), pp. 141–51. Also James Joyce, *A Portrait of the Artist as a Young Man* (Harmondsworth: Penguin, 1970).

14 Friedrich Nietzsche, *Twilight of the Idols*, trans. R. J. Hollingdale (Harmondsworth: Penguin, 1982), p. 38.

15 Hélène Cixous, 'Castration or Decapitation?', trans. A. Kuhn, *Signs*, vol. 7 (1981), 36–55 (p. 55).

16 *Angst* has been translated by J. Levy (London: John Calder, 1985).

17 There is a cassette, available from *des femmes*, of Cixous reading from *Préparatifs*. This cassette is a useful starting point for anyone seeking to explore Cixous's fiction.

18 'Wedding Preparations in the Country', in *The Penguin Complete Stories of Franz Kafka*, ed. N. N. Glatzer (London: Allen Lane, 1983), pp. 52–76 (p. 53).

19 For a helpful discussion of the intertext of *Illa*, see Tilde A. Sankovitch, 'Hélène Cixous: The Pervasive Myth', in *French Women Writers and the Book: Myths of Access and Desire* (Syracuse, New York: Syracuse University Press, 1988), pp. 127–52.

20 Virgil, *Georgics*, trans. J. Dryden (London: Pollock, 1949), IV, 494 ff.

21 A short extract from *Le livre de Promethea* (pp. 97–102) has been translated by S. Sellers and A. Liddle as 'The Last Word', *Women's Review*, no. 6 (1986), 22–4. For an interesting discussion of the subjective complexity of this novel see Sarah Cornell, 'Hélène Cixous's "Le livre de Promethea": Paradise Refound', in S. Sellers (ed.), *Writing Differences: Readings from the Seminar of Hélène Cixous* (Milton Keynes: Open University Press, 1988), pp. 127–40.

For an analysis of the importance of this text in relation to Cixous's work as a whole see Béatrice Slama, 'Entre amour et écriture: "Le livre de Promethea" ', in F. van Rossum-Guyon and M. Diaz-Diocaretz (eds), *Hélène Cixous*, pp. 127–48.

22 P. B. Shelley, 'Prometheus Unbound', in *Shelley*, selected by K. Raine (Harmondsworth: Penguin, 1974), pp. 89–186.

23 See *Un K. incompréhensible: Pierre Goldman* (Paris: Christian Bourgois, 1975).

24 See Nadezhda Mandelshtam, *Hope Against Hope*, trans. M. Hayward (Harmondsworth: Penguin, 1970).

25 Cixous addresses this point in an interview with Françoise van Rossum-Guyon, where she insists that the details of particular political struggles were not her object in *Manne*, but rather the relations between resistance, the poetic, and personal commitment: see F. van Rossum-Guyon and M. Diaz-Diocaretz (eds), *Hélène Cixous*, pp. 213–34. These themes are further developed in Cixous's most recent novel *Jours de l'an* (Paris: des femmes, 1990).

4 STAGING HISTORY

1 Jacques Derrida, 'Différance', in *Margins of Philosophy*, trans. A. Bass (Brighton: Harvester, 1982), pp. 1–27 (p. 9).

2 'Le lieu du crime, le lieu du pardon', in *L'Indiade ou l'Inde de leurs rêves, et quelques écrits sur le théâtre* (Paris: Théâtre du Soleil, 1987), pp. 253–9 (p. 256).

3 'Le chemin de légende', in *Théâtre: Portrait de Dora et La prise de l'école de Madhubaï* (Paris: des femmes, 1986), pp. 7–11 (p. 10).

4 'The Theater of Cruelty and the Closure of Representation', in *Writing and Difference*, trans. A. Bass (London: Routledge & Kegan Paul, 1978), pp. 232–50 (p. 248).

5 'The Theatre and its Double', in *Collected works of Antonin Artaud*, trans. V. Corti, 4 vols (London: Calder & Boyars, 1974), vol. 1, pp. 1–110 (p. 5).

6 'The Theatre and its Double', p. 53.

7 See, for example, Anne-Marie Picard, ' "L'Indiade": Ariane's and Hélène's Conjugate Dreams', *Modern Drama*, vol. 32 (1989), pp. 24–38.

8 'Aller à la mer', *Le Monde*, 28 Apr. 1977, p. 19; translated by B. Kerslake in *Modern Drama*, vol. 27 (1984), 546–8.

9 Cixous's argument here is reminiscent of Laura Mulvey's important discussion of the libidinal economy of filmic representation in 'Visual Pleasure and Narrative Cinema', *Screen*, vol. 16, no. 3 (1975), 6–18.

10 'L'incarnation', in *L'Indiade*, pp. 260–6 (p. 260).

11 'La Pupille', in *Cahiers Renaud-Barrault*, 78 (1971), 3–136 (p. 106).

12 *Théâtre: Portrait de Dora et La Prise de l'école de Madhubaï*, translated by A. Barrows in *Benmussa Directs: Portrait of Dora and The Singular Life of Albert Nobbs* (London: John Calder, 1979).

13 See C. Bernheimer and C. Kahane (eds), *In Dora's Case: Freud–Hysteria–Feminism* (London: Virago, 1985).

14 Simone Benmussa, 'Introduction', in *Benmussa Directs*, pp. 9–26 (p. 12).
15 Hélène Cixous and Catherine Clément, 'Exchange', in *The Newly Born Woman*, trans. B Wing (Manchester: Manchester University Press, 1986), pp. 133–60 (p. 154).
16 See the review of *L'Arrivante* in *Le Monde*, 30 July 1977, p. 14.
17 See D. Grene and R. Lattimore (eds), *Greek Tragedies: Volume One* (London: University of Chicago Press, 1960), 107–76.
18 See Colette Godard, 'Interview with Hélène Cixous', *Le Monde*, 28 July 1978, p. 16.
19 See *Le Nom d'Œdipe* (Paris: des femmes, 1978), p. 74.
20 See *Le Monde*, 'Interview', 28 July 1978. For an analysis of the consequent difficulties presented by *Le Nom d'Œdipe* for feminist theatre practitioners, see Mieke Kolk, 'La vengeance d'Œdipe: Théorie féministe et pratique du théâtre', in F. van Rossum-Guyon and M. Diaz-Diocaretz (eds), *Hélène Cixous: chemins d'une écriture* (Amsterdam: Rodopi, 1990), pp. 177–86.
21 See *Théâtre: Portrait de Dora et La Prise de l'école de Madhubaï*. The play has been translated by D. Carpenter as *The Conquest of the School at Madhubai*, in *Women and Performance*, vol. 3 (1986), 59–96.
22 See Heinrich Von Kleist, 'Michael Kohlhaas', *The Marquise of O., and Other Stories*, trans. M. Greenberg (London: Faber & Faber, 1960), pp. 85–183.
23 B. Brecht, 'Short Description of a New Technique of Acting which Produces an Alienation Effect', in J. Willett (ed.), *Brecht on Theatre* (London: Methuen, 1978), pp. 136–47 (p. 139).
24 See Wolfgang Sohlich, 'The "Théâtre du Soleil's Mephisto" and the Problematics of Political Theatre', *Theatre Journal*, vol. 38 (1986), 137–53.
25 Programme for *Richard II*, cited in D. Bradby, *Modern French Drama 1940–1980* (Cambridge: Cambridge University Press, 1984), p. 213.
26 Véronique Hotte, 'Entretien avec Hélène Cixous', *Théâtre/Public*, 68 (1986), 22–9.
27 Anthony Barnett, 'Cambodia Will Never Disappear', *New Left Review*, no. 180 (1990), 101–25.
28 'L'incarnation', *L'Indiade*, pp. 260–6 (p. 265).
29 'Qui es-tu?', *L'Indiade*, pp. 267–78 (p. 278).
30 See Anne-Marie Picard, ' "L'Indiade" '. It is also interesting to compare the different versions of Act 2, sc. i, that are published in *L'Indiade*, which show the movement between historical detail and symbolic weight, particularly in terms of the character of Gandhi.
31 'L'ourse, la tombe, les étoiles', *L'Indiade*, pp. 247–52.
32 Gustave Flaubert, *Madame Bovary* (Paris: Garnier-Flammarion, 1979), Part 2, chap. 12, p. 219.
33 'C'est l'histoire d'une étoile', *Roméo et Juliette: Le livre*, adapted by G. Robin (Paris: Editions Papiers, 1986), pp. 20–3.

BIBLIOGRAPHY

HELENE CIXOUS: PUBLISHED WORKS IN FRENCH

Le Prénom de Dieu (Paris: Grasset, 1967).
L'Exil de James Joyce ou l'art du remplacement (Paris: Grasset, 1968).
Dedans (Paris: Grasset, 1969); reprinted (Paris: des femmes, 1986).
Les Commencements (Paris: Grasset, 1970).
Le Troisième Corps (Paris: Grasset, 1970).
'Henry James: l'écriture comme placement: ou de l'ambiguïté de l'intérêt', *Poétique*, no. 1 (1970), 35–50.
Un Vrai Jardin (Paris: Herne, 1971).
'Introduction' to Lewis Carroll, *De l'autre côté du miroir; La Chasse au Snark/Through the Looking-Glass; The Hunting of the Snark* (Paris: Aubier-Flammarion, 1971).
'La pupille', *Cahiers Renaud-Barrault*, no. 78 (1971), 3–136.
Neutre (Paris: Grasset, 1972).
'Poe re-lu: une poétique du revenir', *Critique*, no. 299 (1972), 299–327.
Portrait du soleil (Paris: Denoël, 1973).
Tombe (Paris: Seuil, 1973).
'L'essor de plus-je', *L'Arc (Jacques Derrida)*, no. 54 (1973), 46–52.
'L'affiche décolle', *Cahiers Renaud-Barrault*, no. 83 (1973), 27–37.
Prénoms de personne (Paris: Seuil, 1974)
'Introduction' to James Joyce, *Dublinois: Les morts, Contreparties/Dubliners. The Dead, Counterparts* (Paris: Aubier-Flammarion, 1974)
[With Catherine Clément] *La Jeune Née* (Paris: Union Générale d'Editions, 10/18, 1975).
Un K. incompréhensible: Pierre Goldman (Paris: Christian Bourgois, 1975).
Révolutions pour plus d'un Faust (Paris: Seuil, 1975).
'Le rire de la Méduse', *L'Arc (Simone de Beauvoir)*, no. 61 (1975), 39–54.
Souffles (Paris: des femmes, 1975).
[With Michel Foucault] 'A propos de Marguerite Duras', *Cahiers Renaud-Barrault*, no. 89 (1975), 8–22.
'Le paradire (extraits)', *Cahiers Renaud-Barrault*, no. 89 (1975), 110–27.
'Preface' to Phyllis Chesler, *Les Femmes et la folie* (Paris: Payot, 1975).
La (Paris: Gallimard, 1976); reprinted (Paris: des femmes, 1979).
Partie (Paris: des femmes, 1976).

Portrait de Dora (Paris: des femmes, 1976); reprinted (Paris: des femmes, 1986).

'Le sexe ou la tête?', *Les Cahiers du GRIF*, no. 13 (1976), 5–15.

Angst (Paris: des femmes, 1977).

[With Annie Leclerc and Madeleine Gagnon] *La Venue à l'écriture* (Paris: Union Générale d'Editions, 10/18, 1977).

'Aller à la mer', *Le Monde*, 28 Apr. 1977, p. 19.

Le Nom d'Œdipe: chant du corps interdit (Paris: des femmes, 1978).

Préparatifs de noces au-delà de l'abîme (Paris: des femmes, 1978). [This is also available on cassette.]

'Vincennes, héritière de 68, dans le vertige de la scène avec le père', *des femmes en mouvements*, no. 11 (1978), 70–3.

Anankè (Paris: des femmes, 1979).

Vivre l'orange/To Live the Orange, bilingual text, trans. A. Liddle and S. Cornell (Paris: des femmes, 1979).

'Poésie e(s)t politique?', *des femmes en mouvements: hebdo*, no. 4, Nov. Dec. 1979, 29–32.

Illa (Paris: des femmes, 1980).

With ou l'art de l'innocence (Paris: des femmes, 1981).

Limonade tout était si infini (Paris: des femmes, 1982).

Le Livre de Promethea (Paris: Gallimard, 1983).

'12 Août 1980', bilingual text, trans. B. Wing, *Boundary* 2, vol. 12, no. 2 (1984), 8–39.

L'Histoire terrible mais inachevée de Norodom Sihanouk roi du Cambodge (Paris: Théâtre du Soleil, 1985).

Entre l'écriture (Paris: des femmes, 1986).

La Bataille d'Arcachon (Laval, Québec: Trois, 1986).

Théâtre: Portrait de Dora et La Prise de l'école de Madhubaï (Paris: des femmes, 1986).

'La séparation du gâteau', in *Pour Nelson Mandela* (Paris: Gallimard, 1986), pp. 75–93.

'Un fils', in *Hamlet: le livre*, adapted by M. Vitoz (Paris: Editions Papiers, 1986), pp. 9–15.

'C'est l'histoire d'une étoile', in *Roméo et Juliette: le livre*, adapted by G. Robin (Paris: Editions Papiers, 1986), pp. 20–3.

L'Indiade ou l'Inde de leurs rêves; et quelques écrits sur le théâtre (Paris: Théâtre du Soleil, 1987)

Manne: aux Mandelstams aux Mandelas (Paris: des femmes, 1988).

'Marina Tsvetaeva – le feu éteint celle . . . ', *Les Cahiers du GRIF*, no. 39 (1988), 87–96.

L'Heure de Clarice Lispector (Paris: des femmes, 1989).

Jours de l'an (Paris: des femmes, 1990).

'De la scène de l'Inconscient à la scène de l'Histoire', in F. van Rossum-Guyon and M. Diaz-Diocaretz (eds), *Hélène Cixous: chemins d'une écriture* (Amsterdam: Rodopi, 1990), pp. 15–34.

'Clarice Lispector, Marina Tsvetaeva: Autoportraits', in F. van Rossum-Guyon (ed.), *Femmes, Women, Frauen* (Amsterdam: Rodopi, forthcoming).

HELENE CIXOUS: ENGLISH TRANSLATIONS

'The Character of "Character" ', trans. K. Cohen, *New Literary History*, vol. 5 (1974), 383–402.

'At Circe's, or the Self-Opener', trans. C Bové, *Boundary 2*, vol. 3 (1975), 387–97.

The Exile of James Joyce, trans. S. Purcell (London: John Calder, 1976).

'Fiction and its Phantoms: A Reading of Freud's *Das Unheimliche* (The "Uncanny")', trans. R. Dennomé, *New Literary History*, vol. 7 (1976), 525–48.

Portrait of Dora, trans. A. Barrows, in *Benmussa Directs: Portrait of Dora and the Singular Life of Albert Nobbs* (London: John Calder, 1979), pp. 27–67.

'The Laugh of the Medusa', trans. K. and P. Cohen, in Elaine Marks and Isabelle de Courtivron (eds), *New French Feminisms* (Brighton: Harvester, 1980), pp. 254–64.

'Castration or Decapitation?', trans. A. Kuhn, *Signs*, vol. 7 (1981), 36–55.

'Introduction to Lewis Carroll's "Through the Looking Glass" and "The Hunting of the Snark"', trans. M. Maclean, *New Literary History*, vol. 13 (1982), 231–51.

'Aller à la mer', trans. B. Kerslake, *Modern Drama*, 27 (1984), 546–8.

'Joyce: the (R)use of Writing', trans. J. Still, in D. Attridge and D. Ferrer (eds), *Post-Structuralist Joyce: Essays from the French* (Cambridge: Cambridge University Press, 1984), pp. 15–30.

'Reading Clarice Lispector's "Sunday Before going to Sleep"', trans. B. Wing, *Boundary 2*, vol. 12, no. 2 (1984), 41–8.

Angst, trans. J. Levy (London: John Calder, 1985).

Inside, trans. C. Barko (New York: Schocken, 1986).

[With Catherine Clément], *The Newly Born Woman*, trans. B. Wing, Theory and History of Literature Series no. 24 (Manchester: Manchester University Press, 1986).

The Conquest of the School at Madhubai, trans. D Carpenter, *Women and Performance*, vol. 3 (1986), 59–96.

'The Last Word' (Extract from *Le Livre de Promethea*), trans. S. Sellers and A. Liddle, *Women's Review*, no. 6 (1986), 22–4.

'Reaching the Point of Wheat, or A Portrait of the Artist as a Maturing Woman', *New Literary History*, vol. 19 (1987), 1–21.

'Extreme Fidelity', trans. A. Liddle and S. Sellers, in S. Sellers (ed.), *Writing Differences: Readings from the Seminar of Hélène Cixous* (Milton Keynes: Open University Press, 1988), pp. 9–36.

'Tancredi Continues', trans. A. Liddle and S. Sellers, in S. Sellers (ed.), *Writing Differences: Readings from the Seminar of Hélène Cixous* (Milton Keynes: Open University Press, 1988), pp. 37–53.

'The "Double World" of Writing'; 'Listening to the Truth'; 'A Realm of Characters'; 'Writing as a Second Heart', in S. Sellers (ed.), *Delighting the Heart: A Notebook by Women Writers* (London: The Women's Press, 1989), pp. 18; 69; 126–8; 198.

'From the Scene of the Unconscious to the Scene of History', trans. D. Carpenter, *Future Literary History* (1989), 1–8.

Reading With Clarice Lispector, trans. V. Andermatt Conley (London: Harvester Wheatsheaf, 1990).

'Difficult Joys' (paper delivered in English), in Helen Wilcox, Keith McWatters, Ann Thompson and Linda R. Williams (eds), *The Body and the Text: Hélène Cixous, Reading and Teaching* (London: Harvester Wheatsheaf, 1990), pp. 5–30.

'The Name of Oedipus', trans. J. Miller and C. Makward, *Out of Bounds: Women's Theatre in French* (Ann Arbor: University of Michigan, forthcoming).

Her Arrival in Writing, trans. A. Liddle and D. Carpenter-Jensen (Boston: Harvard University Press, forthcoming).

INTERVIEWS WITH HELENE CIXOUS

Collin, Françoise, 'Quelques questions à Hélène Cixous', *Les Cahiers du GRIF*, no. 13 (1976), 16–20.

Makward, Christiane, 'Interview with Hélène Cixous', *Sub-Stance*, no. 13 (1976), 19–37.

Rossum-Guyon, Françoise van, 'Entretien avec Hélène Cixous', *Revue des sciences humaines*, no. 168 (1977), 479–93.

Hotte, Véronique, 'Entretien avec Hélène Cixous', *Théâtre/Public*, no. 68 (1986), 22–9.

Sellers, Susan, 'Hélène Cixous', *Women's Review*, no. 7 (1986), 22–3.

Rossum-Guyon, Françoise van, 'A propos de *Manne*: Entretien avec Hélène Cixous', in F. van Rossum-Guyon and M. Diaz-Diocaretz (eds), *Hélène Cixous: chemins d'une écriture* (Amsterdam: Rodopi, 1990), pp. 213–34.

RELEVANT CRITICAL AND LITERARY TEXTS

Abel, Elizabeth (ed.), *Writing and Sexual Difference* (Brighton: Harvester, 1982).

Aeschylus, The Oresteia, trans. R. Fagles (Harmondsworth: Penguin, 1977).

Albistur, Maïté and Armogathe, Daniel, *Histoire du féminisme français*, 2 vols (Paris: des femmes, 1977–8).

Alexandrescu, Liliana, ' "Norodom Sihanouk": l'inachevé comme lecture shakespearienne de l'Histoire contemporaine', in F. van Rossum-Guyon and M. Diaz-Diocaretz (eds), *Hélène Cixous: chemins d'une écriture* (Amsterdam: Rodopi, 1990), pp. 187–204.

Andrews, C. (ed.), *The Ancient Egyptian Book of the Dead*, trans. R. O. Faulkner (London: British Museum, 1985).

Artaud, Antonin, 'The Theatre and its Double', in *Collected Works of Antonin Artaud*, trans. V. Corti, 4 vols (London: Calder & Boyars, 1974), vol. 1, pp. 1–110.

Bachofen, J.-J. *Das Mutterrecht* (Stuttgart, 1861).

Barnett, Anthony, 'Cambodia Will Never Disappear', *New Left Review*, no. 180 (1990), 101–25.

Barthes, Roland, *Roland Barthes*, trans. R. Howard (London: Macmillan, 1977).

_____ 'Textual Analysis: Poe's "Valdemar"', in D. Lodge (ed.), *Modern Criticism and Theory: A Reader* (London: Longman, 1988), pp. 172–95.

Bataille, Georges, *Le Bleu du ciel* (Paris: Pauvert, 1985).

_____ *The Story of the Eye*, trans. J. Neugroschel (Harmondsworth: Penguin, 1982).

_____ *The Accursed Share: An Essay on General Economy*, trans. R. Hurley, 3 vols, vol. 1 (New York: Zone Books, 1988).

Beall, C. B., *La Fortune du Tasse en France*, Studies in Literature and Philology no. 4 (Eugene, Oregon: University of Oregon Press, 1942).

Benjamin, Walter, *Charles Baudelaire: A Lyric Poet in the Era of High Capitalism*, trans. H. Zohn (London: NLB, 1973).

Bernal, Martin, *Black Athena: The Afroasiatic Roots of Classical Civilization*, vol. 1 (London: Free Association Books, 1987).

Bernheimer, C. and Kahane, C. (eds), *In Dora's Case: Freud–Hysteria–Feminism* (London: Virago, 1985).

Bourdieu, Pierre, *L'Ontologie politique de Martin Heidegger* (Paris: Minuit, 1975, repr. 1988).

Bradby, David, *Modern French Drama 1940–1980* (Cambridge: Cambridge University Press, 1984).

Brennan, Teresa (ed)., *Between Feminism and Psychoanalysis* (London: Routledge, 1989).

Burton, Richard D. E., 'The Unseen Seer or Proteus in the City: Aspects of a Nineteenth Century Parisian Myth', *French Studies*, vol. 42, no. 1 (1988), 50–68.

Caws, Mary Ann, *Reading Frames in Modern Fiction* (Princeton: Princeton University Press, 1985).

Cobb, Palmer, *The Influence of E. T. A. Hoffmann on the Tales of Edgar Allan Poe*, Studies in Philology, vol. III (Chapel Hill: University of North Carolina Press, 1908).

Cohn, Ruby, 'Ariane Mnouchkine: Playwright of a Collective', in E. Brater (ed.), *Feminine Focus: The New Women Playwrights* (Oxford: Oxford University Press, 1989).

Conley, Verena Andermatt, *Hélène Cixous: Writing the Feminine* (Lincoln, Nebraska: University of Nebraska Press, 1984).

_____ 'Approaches', *Boundary 2*, vol. 12, no. 2 (1984), 1–7.

_____ 'Introduction' to *Reading With Clarice Lispector* (London: Harvester Wheatsheaf, 1990), pp. vii–xviii.

Cornell, Sarah, 'Hélène Cixous's "Le livre de Promethea": Paradise Refound', in S. Sellers (ed.), *Writing Differences: Readings from the Seminar of Hélène Cixous* (Milton Keynes: Open University Press, 1988), pp. 127–40.

_____ 'Hélène Cixous and "Les Etudes Féminines" ' in H. Wilcox, Keith McWatters, Ann Thompson, Linda R. Williams (eds), *The*

Body and The Text: Hélène Cixous, Reading and Teaching (London: Harvester Wheatsheaf, 1990), pp. 31–40.

Crecelius, Kathryn J., 'La voix de Tancrède: de Cixous à Sand', in F. van Rossum-Guyon and M. Diaz-Diocaretz (eds), *Hélène Cixous: chemins d'une écriture* (Amsterdam: Rodopi, 1990), pp. 75–82.

Dante Alighieri, *The Divine Comedy*, trans J.D. Sinclair, 3 vols (New York: Oxford University Press, 1981).

Defromont, Françoise, 'Metaphorical Thinking and Poetic Writing in Virginia Woolf and Hélène Cixous' in H. Wilcox, Keith McWatters, Ann Thompson, Linda R. Williams (eds), *The Body and The Text: Hélène Cixous, Reading and Teaching* (London: Harvester Wheatsheaf, 1990), pp. 114–25.

—— 'L'épopée du corps', in F. van Rossum-Guyon and M. Diaz-Diocaretz (eds), *Hélène Cixous: chemins d'une écriture* (Amsterdam: Rodopi, 1990), pp. 91–8.

Deleuze, Gilles, *Logique du sens* (Paris: Union Générale d'Editions, 1968).

—— 'Hélène Cixous ou l'écriture stroboscopique', *Le Monde*, 11 Aug. 1972, p. 10.

—— *Nietzsche and Philosophy*, trans. H. Tomlinson (London: Athlone Press, 1983).

Delphy, Christine, *Close to Home: A Materialist Analysis of Women's Oppression* (London: Hutchinson, 1984).

Derrida, Jacques, 'The Purveyor of Truth', *Yale French Studies*, 52 (1975), 31–113.

—— *Writing and Difference*, trans. A. Bass (London: Routledge & Kegan Paul, 1978).

—— *Margins of Philosophy*, trans. A. Bass (Brighton: Harvester, 1982).

—— *Dissemination*, trans. B. Johnson (London: Athlone, 1981).

—— *Glas*, trans. J. P. Leavey and R. Rand (London: University of Nebraska Press, 1986).

—— *The Post Card*, trans. A. Bass (London: University of Chicago Press, 1987).

—— 'Devant la loi', in A. Phillips Griffiths (ed.), *Philosophy and Literature*, Royal Institute of Philosophy Lecture Series no. 16 (Cambridge: Cambridge University Press, 1984), pp. 173–88.

Diamond, Elin, 'Benmussa's Adaptations: Unauthorized Texts from Elsewhere', in E. Brater (ed.), *Feminine Focus: The New Women Playwrights* (Oxford: Oxford University Press, 1989), pp. 64–78.

Duchen, Claire, *Feminism in France From May '68 to Mitterand* (London: Routledge & Kegan Paul, 1986).

—— (ed.), *French Connections: Voices from the Women's Movement in France* (London: Hutchinson, 1987).

Eisenstein, Hester and Jardine, Alice A. (eds), *The Future of Difference* (New York: Barnard College Women's Center, 1980).

Eliot, T. S., *From Poe to Valéry* (New York: Harcourt, Brace, 1948).

Engels, F., *The Origin of the Family, Private Property and the State*, Introduction by Michele Barrett (Harmondsworth: Penguin, 1985).

152

Ertel, Evelyne, 'Entre l'imitation et la transposition', *Théâtre/Public*, no. 68 (1986), 25–9.

Etcheson, Craig, *The Rise and Demise of Democratic Kampuchea* (London: Frances Pinter, 1984).

Evans, Martha Noel, *Masks of Tradition: Women and the Politics of Writing in Twentieth-century France* (London: Cornell University Press, 1987).

Farias, Victor, *Heidegger et le nazisme* (Paris: Verdier, 1987).

Finas, Lucette, 'Le pourpre du neutre', in *Le Bruit d'Iris* (Paris: Flammarion, 1978), pp. 303–23.

Fisher, Claudine Guégan, *La Cosmogonie d'Hélène Cixous* (Amsterdam: Rodopi, 1988).

Foye, R. (ed.), *The Unknown Poe* (San Francisco: City Lights, 1980).

Freeman, Barbara, 'Plus corps donc plus écriture: Hélène Cixous and the Mind–Body Problem', *Paragraph*, vol. 11, no. 1 (1988), 58–70.

Freud, Sigmund, 'Fragment of an Analysis of a Case of Hysteria ['Dora']', *The Standard Edition of the Complete Psychological Works of Sigmund Freud*, ed. J. Strachey, 24 vols (London: Hogarth, 1953–74) [=*SE*], vol. 7, pp. 3–122.

————— 'Delusion and Dreams in Jensen's "Gradiva"', *SE*, vol. 9, pp. 7–95.

————— 'Leonardo Da Vinci and a Memory of his Childhood', *SE*, vol. 11, pp. 59–137.

————— 'The Uncanny', *SE*, vol. 17, pp. 217–52.

————— 'Beyond the Pleasure Principle', *SE*, vol. 18, pp. 7–64.

————— 'Female Sexuality', *SE*, vol. 21, 221–43.

————— 'Moses and Monotheism', *SE*, vol. 23, pp. 7–137.

Genet, Jean, *The Thief's Journal*, trans. B. Frechtman (Harmondsworth: Penguin, 1967).

————— *The Maids*, trans. B. Frechtman (London: Faber, 1963)

Gallop, Jane, *The Daughter's Seduction: Feminism and Psychoanalysis* (London: Macmillan, 1982).

————— *Reading Lacan* (London: Cornell University Press, 1985).

————— '"Writing and Sexual Difference": The Difference Within', in E. Abel (ed.), *Writing and Sexual Difference* (Brighton: Harvester, 1982), pp. 283–90.

Goldhill, Simon, *Language, Sexuality, Narrative: The "Oresteia"* (Cambridge: Cambridge University Press, 1984).

————— *Reading Greek Tragedy*, (Cambridge: Cambridge University Press, 1986).

H.D., *Helen in Egypt* (Manchester: Carcanet, 1985).

Hanrahan, Mairéad, 'Une porte du "Portrait du soleil" ou la succulence du sujet', in F. van Rossum-Guyon and M. Diaz-Diocaretz (eds), *Hélène Cixous: chemins d'une écriture* (Amsterdam: Rodopi, 1990), pp. 45–53.

Harrison, Nancy, *Winnie Mandela: Mother of a Nation* (London: Victor Gollancz, 1985).

Heath, Stephen, 'Difference', *Screen*, vol. 19, no. 3 (1978), 51–112.

Hegel, G. W. F., *Phenomenology of Spirit*, trans. A. V. Miller (Oxford: Clarendon Press, 1979).

Heidegger, Martin, *Being and Time*, trans. J. Macquarrie and E. Robinson (Oxford: Basil Blackwell, 1978).

—— *Poetry, Language, Thought*, trans. A. Hofstadter (New York: Harper & Row, 1971).

Hertz, Neil, 'Freud and the Sandman', in J. V. Harari (ed.), *Textual Strategies*, (London: Methuen, 1980), pp. 296–321.

Hobson, Marian, 'Deconstruction, Empiricism, and the Postal Services', *French Studies*, vol. 36 (1982), 290–314.

Hoffmann, E.T.A., *Tales of Hoffmann*, ed. R. J. Hollingdale (Harmondsworth: Penguin, 1982).

—— *Selected Writings*, ed. L. J. Kent and E. C. Knight, 2 vols (London: University of Chicago Press, 1969).

—— 'Kreisleriana', in *Fantaisies dans la manière de Callot*, trans. H. de Curzon (Paris: Phébus, 1979), pp. 47–97 and 361–412.

Huyssen, Andreas, *After the Great Divide: Modernism, Mass Culture, Postmodernism* (Bloomington: Indiana University Press, 1986).

Irigaray, Luce, *Ce sexe qui n'en est pas un* (Paris: Minuit, 1977).

—— *L'Éthique de la différence sexuelle* (Paris: Minuit, 1984).

Jardine, Alice A., *Gynesis: Configurations of Woman and Modernity* (London: Cornell University Press, 1985).

—— 'In the name of the modern: feminist questions *d'après gynesis'*, in S. Sheridan (ed.), *Grafts: Feminist Cultural Criticism* (London: Verso, 1988), pp. 157–91.

Jensen, Wilhelm, 'Gradiva: A Pompeiian Fancy', in S. Freud, *Delusion and Dream*, trans. H. M. Downey (London: George Allen & Unwin, 1921), pp. 12–108.

Jentsch, E., 'Zur Psychologie des unheimlichen', *Psychiatrisch-neurologische Wochenschrift*, 8, 195 (1906), 219–21, 226–7.

Johnson, Barbara, *The Critical Difference: Essays in the Contemporary Rhetoric of Reading* (London: Johns Hopkins University Press, 1980).

Jones, Anne Rosalind, 'Writing the Body: Towards an Understanding of l'écriture féminine', in E. Showalter (ed.), *The New Feminist Criticism* (London: Virago, 1985), pp. 361–77.

Jouve, Nicole Ward, *White Woman Speaks with Forked Tongue: Criticism as Autobiography* (London: Routledge, 1990).

—— 'Oranges et sources: Colette et Hélène Cixous', in F. van Rossum-Guyon and M. Diaz-Diocaretz (eds), *Hélène Cixous: chemins d'une écriture* (Amsterdam: Rodopi, 1990), pp. 55–73.

Joyce, James, *A Portrait of the Artist as a Young Man* (Harmondsworth: Penguin, 1970).

Kafka, Franz, *The Trial* (Harmondsworth: Penguin, 1975).

—— *The Penguin Complete Short Stories of Franz Kafka*, ed. N. N. Glatzer (London: Allen Lane, 1983).

Kālidasa, 'Śakuntalā', in M. Coulson (ed.), *Three Sanskrit Plays* (Harmondsworth: Penguin, 1981), pp. 29–161.

Kierkegaard, Søren, *A Kierkegaard Anthology*, ed. R. Bretall (Princeton: Princeton University Press, 1946).

Kleist, Heinrich Von, *The Marquise of O., and Other Stories*, trans. M. Greenberg (London: Faber & Faber, 1960).

—— *Heinrich Von Kleist: Plays*, ed. W. Hinderer (New York: Continuum, 1982).

—— 'About the Marionette Theatre', *Life and Letters Today*, vol. 16 (1937), 101–5.

Kolk, Mieke, 'La vengeance d'Œdipe: théorie féministe et pratique du théâtre', in F. van Rossum-Guyon and M. Diaz-Diocaretz (eds), *Hélène Cixous: chemins d'une écriture* (Amsterdam: Rodopi, 1990), pp. 177–86.

Kristeva, Julia, *Revolution in Poetic Language*, trans. M. Waller (New York: Columbia University Press, 1984).

Kuhn, Annette, 'Introduction to Hélène Cixous's "Castration or Decapitation?"', *Signs*, vol. 7, no. 1 (1981), pp. 36–40.

La Nouvelle Critique, 'Dossier Femmes', no. 116 (1978), 2–52.

Lacan, J., *Ecrits* (Paris: Editions du Seuil, 1966).

—— *Le Séminaire: Livre XX, Encore*, ed. J.-A. Miller (Paris: Editions du Seuil, 1975). ['Dieu et la jouissance de Là femme', trans. J. Rose, in J. Mitchell and J. Rose (eds), *Jacques Lacan and the 'école freudienne'* (London: Macmillan, 1982), pp. 137–48].

Lacoue-Labarthe, Philippe, *Heidegger, Art and Politics: The Fiction of the Political*, trans. C. Turner (Oxford: Basil Blackwell, 1990).

Lamont, Rosette C., 'The Reverse Side of a Portrait: The Dora of Freud and Cixous', in E. Brater (ed.), *Feminine Focus: The New Women Playwrights* (Oxford: Oxford University Press, 1989), pp. 79–93.

Leclerc, Annie, *Parole de femme* (Paris: Grasset, 1974).

Les Temps Modernes, 'Les femmes s'entêtent', nos 333–4 (1974).

Lie, Sissel, 'Pour une lecture féminine?' in Helen Wilcox, Keith McWatters, Ann Thompson and Linda R. Williams (eds), *The Body and The Text: Hélène Cixous, Reading and Teaching* (London: Harvester Wheatsheaf, 1990), pp. 196–203.

Lispector, Clarice, *La Passion selon G.H.* (Paris: des femmes, 1985).

—— *The Apple in the Dark*, trans. G. Rabassa (London: Virago, 1985).

—— *Où étais-tu pendant la nuit?* (Paris: des femmes, 1985).

—— *The Hour of the Star*, trans. G. Pontiero (Manchester: Carcanet, 1986).

—— *The Foreign Legion: Stories and Chronicles*, trans. G. Pontiero (Manchester: Carcanet, 1986).

—— *Near to the Wild Heart*, trans. G. Pontiero (Manchester: Carcanet, 1990).

Lloyd, Rosemary, *Baudelaire et Hoffmann: affinités et influences* (Cambridge: Cambridge University Press, 1979).

Lyotard, Jean-François, *Heidegger et 'les juifs'* (Paris: Galilée, 1988).

MacCabe, Colin, *James Joyce and the Revolution of the Word* (London: Macmillan, 1978).

Makward, Christiane, 'Structures du silence/du délire: Duras et Cixous', *Poétique*, no. 35 (1978), 314–24.

Mandelshtam, Osip, *The Eyesight of Wasps: Poems*, trans. J. Greene (London: Angel Books, 1989).

——— *50 Poems*, trans. B. Meares (New York: Persea Books, 1977).

Mandelshtam, Nadezhda, *Hope against Hope*, trans. M. Hayward (Harmondsworth: Penguin, 1975).

Marks, Elaine and Courtivron, Isabelle de (eds), *New French Feminisms* (Brighton: Harvester, 1980).

Mauss, Marcel, *The Gift: The Form and Reason for Exchange in Archaic Societies*, trans. W. D. Halls (London: Routledge, 1990).

Miller, Judith G., 'Jean Cocteau and Hélène Cixous: Oedipus', in J. Redmond (ed.), *Drama, Sex and Politics*, Themes in Drama no. 7 (Cambridge: Cambridge University Press, 1985), pp. 203–11.

——— 'Contemporary Women's Voices in French Theatre', *Modern Drama*, vol. 32, no. 1 (1989), 5–23.

Mnouchkine, Ariane, 'L'œuvre de tous', *L'Arc (Brecht)*, no. 55 (1973), 41–4.

——— 'Le besoin d'une forme', *Théâtre/Public*, nos 46–7 (1982), 8–11.

Moi, Toril, *Sexual/Textual Politics: Feminist Literary Theory* (London: Methuen, 1985).

——— (ed), *The Kristeva Reader* (Oxford: Basil Blackwell, 1986).

——— (ed.), *French Feminist Thought: A Reader* (Oxford: Basil Blackwell, 1987).

Morice, Jean, *Cambodge: du sourire à l'horreur* (Paris: France-Empire, 1977).

Moss, Jane, 'Women's Theater in France', *Signs*, vol. 12 (1987), 548–67.

Mounier, C., 'Deux créations collectives du Théâtre du Soleil', in D. Bablet and J. Jacquot (eds), *Les Voies de la création théâtrale* (Paris: CNRS, 1977), pp. 121–278.

Muller, J. P. and Richardson, W. J. (eds), *The Purloined Poe: Lacan, Derrida and Psychoanalytic Reading* (London: Johns Hopkins University Press, 1988).

Mulvey, Laura, 'Visual Pleasure and Narrative Cinema', *Screen*, vol. 16, no. 3 (1975), 6–18.

Nietzsche, Friedrich, *The Birth of Tragedy and The Case of Wagner*, trans. W. Kaufmann (New York: Vintage Books, 1967).

——— *The Gay Science*, trans. W. Kaufmann (New York: Vintage, 1974).

——— *Thus Spoke Zarathustra*, trans. R. J. Hollingdale (Harmondsworth: Penguin, 1969).

——— *A Nietzsche Reader*, ed. R. J. Hollingdale (Harmondsworth: Penguin, 1977).

——— *Twilight of the Idols*, trans. R. J. Hollingdale (Harmondsworth: Penguin, 1982).

Osborne, Milton, *Politics and Power in Cambodia: The Sihanouk Years* (Camberwell, Victoria: Longman, 1973).

Osborne, Richard, *Rossini* (London: Dent, 1986).

Picard, Anne-Marie, ' "L'Indiade": Ariane's and Hélène's Conjugate Dreams', *Modern Drama*, vol. 32 (1989), 24–38.

Poe, Edgar Allan, *Tales of Mystery and Imagination* (London: Dent, 1963).

_____ 'The Philosophy of Composition', in *Works*, 17 vols (New York: AMS Press, 1965), vol. 14, pp. 193–208.

_____ *Oeuvres en prose*, trans. C. Baudelaire, ed. Y.-G. Le Dantec (Paris: Gallimard, Pléiade, 1956).

Ponchaud, François, *Cambodia Year Zero*, trans. N. Amphoux (London: Allen Lane, 1978).

Rabaut, Jean, *Histoire des féminismes français* (Paris: Stock, 1978).

Reader, Keith, *Intellectuals and the Left in France since 1968* (London: Macmillan, 1987).

Richman, Michèle, 'Sex and Signs: The Language of French Feminist Criticism', *Language and Style*, vol. 13, no. 4 (1980), 62–80.

Roberts, Julian, *German Philosophy: An Introduction* (Cambridge: Polity, 1988).

Rossum-Guyon, Françoise van and Diaz-Diocaretz, M. (eds), *Hélène Cixous: chemins d'une écriture* (Amsterdam: Rodopi, 1990).

Running-Johnson, Cynthia, 'Feminine Writing and its Theatrical "Other" ', in J. Redmond (ed.), *Women in Theatre*, Themes in Drama no. 11, (Cambridge: Cambridge University Press, 1989), pp. 177–84.

Said, Edward W., *Orientalism* (London: Routledge & Kegan Paul, 1978).

Salesne, Pierre, 'Hélène Cixous's "Ou l'art de l'innocence": The Path to You', in S. Sellers (ed)., *Writing Differences: Readings from the Seminar of Hélène Cixous* (Milton Keynes: Open University Press, 1988), pp. 113–26.

Sankovitch, Tilde A., 'Hélène Cixous: The Pervasive Myth', in *French Women Writers and the Book: Myths of Access and Desire* (Syracuse, New York: Syracuse University Press, 1988), pp. 127–52.

Savona, Jeannette Laillou, 'In Search of a Feminist Theatre: "Portrait of Dora" ', in E. Brater (ed.), *Feminine Focus: The New Women Playwrights* (Oxford: Oxford University Press, 1989), pp. 94–108.

Sellers, Susan (ed.), *Writing Differences: Readings from the Seminar of Hélène Cixous* (Milton Keynes: Open University Press, 1988).

Semaine de la Pensée Marxiste, *Les Femmes aujourd'hui, demain* (Paris: Editions Sociales, 1975).

Shawcross, William, *Sideshow: Kissinger, Nixon and the Destruction of Cambodia* (London: André Deutsch, 1979).

Shelley, P. B., 'Prometheus Unbound', in *Shelley*, selected by K. Raine (Harmondsworth: Penguin, 1974), pp. 89–186.

Slama, Béatrice, 'Entre amour et écriture: "Le livre de Promethéa" ', in F. van Rossum-Guyon and M. Diaz-Diocaretz (eds), *Hélène Cixous: chemins d'une écriture* (Amsterdam: Rodopi, 1990), pp. 127–48.

Sohlich, Wolfgang, 'The "Théâtre du Soleil's Mephisto" and the Problematics of Political Theatre', *Theatre Journal*, vol. 38 (1986), 137–53.

Sophocles, *Electra*, in *Greek Tragedies: Volume Two*, ed. D. Grene and R. Lattimore (London: University of Chicago Press, 1960), pp. 45–109.

_____ *Oedipus the King*, in *Greek Tragedies: Volume One*, ed. D. Grene and R. Lattimore (London: University of Chicago Press, 1960), pp. 107–76.

Spivak, Gayatri Chakravorty, 'French Feminism in an International Frame', *Yale French Studies*, 62 (1981), 154–84.

Stanton, Domna C., 'Language and Revolution: The Franco-American Dis-Connection', in H. Eisenstein and A. A. Jardine (eds), *The Future of Difference* (New York: Barnard College Women's Center, 1980), pp. 73–87.

——— 'Difference on Trial: A Critique of the Maternal Metaphor in Cixous, Irigaray, and Kristeva', in N. K. Miller (ed.), *The Poetics of Gender* (New York: Columbia University Press, 1986), pp. 157–82.

Stevens, Crista, 'Hélène Cixous: portraying the feminine', in L. Brouwer *et al.* (eds), *Beyond Limits* (Groningen: University of Groningen, 1990), pp. 83–96.

Still, Judith, 'A Feminine Economy: Some Preliminary Thoughts', in Helen Wilcox, Keith McWatters, Ann Thompson and Linda R. Williams (eds), *The Body and the Text: Hélène Cixous, Reading and Teaching* (London: Harvester Wheatsheaf, 1990), pp. 49–60.

Tasso, Torquato, *Jerusalem Delivered*, trans. E. Fairfax (London: Centaur, 1962).

The Arabian Nights' Entertainments (Edinburgh: W. P. Nimmo, 1865).

The Epic of Gilgamish, trans. R. Campbell Thompson (London, 1928).

Tocqueville, Alexis de, *On Democracy, Revolution and Society*, ed. J. Stone and S. Mennell (London: University of Chicago Press, 1980).

Travail Théâtral (supplément), *Différent: Le Théâtre du Soleil* (1976).

Tristan, Anne and de Pisan, Annie, *Histoires du MLF* (Paris: Calmann-Levy, 1977).

Tsvetaeva, Marina, *A Captive Spirit: Selected Prose*, ed. J. Marin King (London: Virago, 1983).

Virgil, *The Georgics*, trans. J. Dryden (London: Pollock, 1949).

Whitford, Margaret, 'Luce Irigaray and the Female Imaginary: Speaking as a Woman', *Radical Philosophy*, 43 (1986), 3–8.

Wilcox, Helen, McWatters, Keith, Thompson, Ann, and Williams, Linda R. (eds), *The Body and the Text: Hélène Cixous, Reading and Teaching* (London: Harvester Wheatsheaf, 1990).

Willett, John (ed.), *Brecht on Theatre* (London: Methuen, 1978).

Willis, Sharon, 'Hélène Cixous's "Portrait de Dora": The Unseen and the Un-Scene', *Theatre Journal*, vol. 37 (1985), 287–301.

INDEX

1) Reading 2) Working p. 9 = stroboscopic reading (*pleasure* on Cixous) p.

invention = 69 (+ myth)

myth = 12-15 ; 85; 94 (ambiguity of myth); 100 (as resource) :